W9-ASI-451

Cooking for a Healthy Church

A Blessing

The silver rain, the shining sun

The fields where scarlet poppies run

And all the ripples of the wheat

Are in the bread that we do eat.

So when we sit and have a meal

And say a grace, we always feel

That we are eating rain and sun

And fields where scarlet poppies run.

Blessings on the meal.

Amen.

Cooking for a Healthy Church

Easy and Nutritious Recipes for the Parish Hall or the Family Table

Collected by Members of
The Episcopal Church Medical Trust

Morehouse Publishing
NEW YORK · HARRISBURG · DENVER

Copyright © 2012 by The Episcopal Church Medical Trust

All rights reserved. No part of this book may be reproduced, stored in a retrieval system, or transmitted in any form or by any means, electronic or mechanical, including photocopying, recording, or otherwise, without the written permission of the publisher.

Unless otherwise noted, the Scripture quotations contained herein are from the New Revised Standard Version Bible, copyright © 1989 by the Division of Christian Education of the National Council of Churches of Christ in the U.S.A. Used by permission. All rights reserved.

The material in this book is for informational purposes only and is not a substitute for professional nutritional or medical advice or treatment. Always seek the advice of a health care professional with any questions about your personal health care status, and prior to making changes in your diet. You should carefully read all information provided by the manufacturers of any ingredients found in this book before using such ingredients. The Episcopal Church Medical Trust and its affiliates expressly disclaim any and all liability for any adverse reactions you, any member of your family, or any other person might experience as a result of contact with or consumption of any ingredients or foods included in this book.

Morehouse Publishing, 4775 Linglestown Road, Harrisburg, PA 17112

Morehouse Publishing, 445 Fifth Avenue, New York, NY 10016

Morehouse Publishing is an imprint of Church Publishing Incorporated.

www.churchpublishing.org

Cover design by Laurie Klein Westhafer
Typeset by Beth Oberholtzer

Library of Congress Cataloging-in-Publication Data

Cooking for a healthy church : easy and nutritious recipes for the parish hall or the family table / collected by members of the Episcopal Church Medical Trust.

    p.   cm.

    ISBN 978-0-8192-2760-7 (pbk.) – ISBN 978-0-8192-2761-4 (ebook)

    1. Cooking. 2. Nutrition. 3. Health promotion–United States. 4. Episcopal Church. Medical Trust. I. Episcopal Church. Medical Trust.

TX714.C65432175 2012

613.2--dc23

2012012307

Printed in the United States of America

12 13 14 15 16 17   10 9 8 7 6 5 4 3 2 1

Contents

Foreword

In 2005, the Episcopal Church Medical Trust began publishing *Health & Wellness News*, a monthly newsletter, as a way to educate our health plan members about various illnesses and management of these medical conditions. The first "healthy" recipes began to appear in print in March 2009, and as the focus of our newsletter shifted from information on illnesses to the promotion of healthy lifestyles, that first recipe became a regular monthly column later that same year. As part of my role in the medical trust, I provide "healthy lifestyle" presentations at meetings throughout the various dioceses, as well as at *Planning for Tomorrow* conferences sponsored by the Church Pension Fund. During these sessions, I often hear from clergy about how difficult it is to maintain a healthy diet because of frequent "potluck dinners" or conferences where food choices were more "comfort" than "healthy."

A bishop once told me that at coffee hours, he tries to stand as far away from the tables as possible so as to not be tempted by the high calorie foods offered. He then said, no matter where I stand, some kind person will fill a plate for me so that I won't be hungry. Rather than appear rude, he decides to eat whatever delicacies appear on the plate. Thus, he is often conflicted between trying to eat healthy, and eating high-calorie foods that he really doesn't want to eat, but does.

As I traveled around from diocese to diocese attending conferences and meetings, it became clear that many of these meals were less than healthful. Don't get me wrong, much of it was delicious, but depending on the locale or the event, there were times when there were no "healthful" choices available. Over the years, I'm glad to say that I have seen a gradual change toward healthier menus.

When we first began discussing the possibility of asking our health plan members to submit recipes for a healthy cookbook, I jokingly suggested the title of the cookbook be *Please Don't Kill the Priest*. Everyone tries to make their best dish to take to a potluck lunch or dinner. These dishes are made with love and care, and are intended to nourish the souls at each of the gatherings—which sometimes means the recipes are full of "not so healthful" ingredients. The aim of this cookbook is to provide recipes for healthful dishes from coffee hour to potluck dinners, as well as for meals in your home.

As people began sending in their recipes, we found that there were some very healthy ones among them. We also received a lot of recipes that were not as healthy. We worked with our nutritionist, who showed us how to lighten the recipes and decrease some of the fat and sugar they contained. However, there were some that were just too rich to be considered for the final publication.

We thank everyone who submitted recipes and/or prayers for this cookbook. It is truly a cookbook for the church, by the church. It is a chance to promote healthy meals for those who work for and serve the church and is a step in promoting a culture of health within, so that all will be *Well to Serve*.

Faithfully,
Libby Miller

Acknowledgments

We would like to thank the following participants for submitting their wonderful recipes:

Adelene Burlington, Adelle Davis, Alexandra Zepeda, Alison Pollock, Andrea Johnson, Ann Armstrong, Ann Bishop Knight, Anne Cooper, Anne Peterson Burke, Anthony F. Chiffolo, Barb Hagen, Barbara Carton-Riker, Bingham Powell, Brenda M. Kolb, Calvin Davis, Carol Foose, Carolyn Enlow, Christine Zeller-Powell, Christy Campbell, Colleen Whepley, Corky Bonesteel, Cynthia Masick, Dhushyanthy Jayawardena, Dorothy Powell, Dr. Elizabeth Sauter, MD, Dr. Lorriane Davis, Elaine Barnwell, Elaine Holt, Elizabeth Gayle, Elizabeth McInnis, Elsie Campbell, Emily McNeil, Evelyn Taft, Evie Foulkes, Gail Myers, Gail S. Myers, Giff Blaylock, GK Chesterton, Helen Goodpaster Rogers, Jane Story Bost, Janelee Wise, Jennifer Boyle, Jenny Martindale, Jerry Ulrich, JoAnn Goetz, John A. Rollins, John Talbott, Joyce Anderson Jackson, Judy Fine, Judy Taylor, Julie Marie Ford, Karen Belson, Karloyn Bowles, Kate Muir, Laura Queen, Libby Miller, Margaret Hall, Marilyn Morrow, Marqua Brunette, Martha Littlejohn, Mary Lowry, Mary Taylor, Meg Gilman King, Meg B. Walker, Mrs. John M. Barr, Mrs. Richard Bennet, Nadene Mathes, Nancy Fisher, Nancy Walker, Patricia Eggenschiller, Patricia Thomson Sauer, Patricia Wareing, Phyllis Hockley, Regina Paleau, Richard Copeland, Rose Rasmus, Rusty Hesse, Ruth Taylor, Sally Leonard, Sandy Davis, Shirley Wehrs, Sister Diana, Sister June Thomas, Sisters of the Society of the Transfiguration, Stephen Wiggin, Su Hadden, Sue Ryan, Sue Welles, The Rev. A. Sam, The Rev. Anne L.Y Manson, The Rev. Bert Hatch, The Rev. Bill Shiflet, The Rev. Bob, The Rev. Bob Wilt, The Rev. Charles Hensel, The Rev. Deacon Mary Beth Emerson, The Rev. Dr. Bill Doggett, The Rev. Dr. Leon Spencer, The Rev. Dr. Nina George-Hacker, The Rev. Dr. Rayner W Hesse Jr., The Rev. Elizabeth Tesi, The Rev. Frank Carson Knebel, The Rev. Gregory Mansfield, The Rev. J. Barrett Miller, The Rev. Jane Flaherty, The Rev. Mary Canavan, The Rev. Melanie Barbarito, The Rev. Michael D. Moore, The Rev. Paul St. Germain, The Rev. Richard Clark, The Rev. Robert Warren Cromey, The Rev. Scott West, The Rev. Steven Jacobson, The Rev. W. Gedge Gayle Jr., The Rev. Wendy Salisbury Howe, The Very Rev. Ronald Clingenpeel, Tony E. Hamby, Vicki Perkins, Victoria Turner, Wesley Emerson, William Morris, William Riker.

Nutritionist's Note

Every meal is an opportunity to nourish our bodies and provide ourselves with the health and energy to do the things we love, and serve the people we care about most. This book is full of recipes submitted by people like you. We kept many of the recipes "as is," but made adjustments where we thought we could enhance the nutrition. We also highlighted the healthier aspects of each recipe and focused on a particular food's health benefit when appropriate.

As a nutritionist, I was trained to design menus based on balancing carbohydrates, fats, and proteins. Today, there is much confusion around food and eating. Questions arise, such as, should we combine carbohydrates and proteins? Can we eat after 8:00 pm? Can eating meat be healthy? Unfortunately, these types of questions distract us from actually eating healthier, but we won't tackle them here; instead, we'll focus on the wonderful food God provided for us and how to simply include them into our busy lives, as we fulfill our calling.

We seem to thrive when we eat as God intended: a diet featuring more vegetables, legumes, fruit, nuts, seeds, fish, and lean meat, if we choose to eat meat. We suggest buying organic when possible, as it appears to be more sustainable for the earth. Avoid processed food in boxes and cans when possible, and eat food as close to its natural state when you can.

We also wanted to make the balance of carbohydrate, fats, and protein more meaningful to you, so we have provided the grams and calories in each dish, as well as the total calories. The distribution of calories from food is a controversial topic, but a simple rule of thumb is to get about 40 percent of your calories from carbohydrates, 30 percent from protein, and 30 percent from fat. So if you eat a food that has 100 total calories per serving; 40 calories would come from fat, 30 from protein, and 30 from fat.

We hope you enjoy serving these recipes to the people you serve and care about in the course of your day and lives.

—Peter K., MS, PT

BREAKFAST

Eat breakfast like a king,

Lunch like a prince,

and dinner like a pauper.

Adelle Davis, nutritionist (1904–1974)

French Toast

Serves 4 (Serving Size: 1 1/2 slices)

French toast is one dish that doesn't really need a recipe. You simply dip slices of bread in a mixture of beaten eggs and milk, and then fry the slices until the outsides turn a nice golden brown color with crisp edges. The insides remain wonderfully soft.

French toast recipes are also very accommodating to the adventurous cook. You can add spices to the egg and milk mixture—like cinnamon and vanilla extract, but others use nutmeg, orange or lemon zests. Using skim milk in place of whole milk or half and half lowers the calorie and fat content of this dish.

Forget the squishy white breads. Whole wheat bread is healthier and has more flavor, but you may use cinnamon raisin or whatever hearty breads you have lying around. It actually helps to use day-old bread so that it will soak up the batter without falling apart. Add fresh berries, slices of peaches or bananas. Start enjoying with this basic recipe:

INGREDIENTS:

3 large eggs
3/4 cup skim milk
pinch of salt
1/4 teaspoon pure vanilla extract
1/4 teaspoon ground cinnamon
6 slices of light whole wheat bread
1 tablespoon of extra virgin olive oil

RECIPE:

In a large bowl, whisk together the eggs, milk, salt, cinnamon, and vanilla extract. Dip both sides of each slice of bread into the batter mixture. Heat oil in a large, non-stick frying pan, over medium heat. To check if the pan is ready, see if a drop of water sizzles on its surface. Fry the slices of bread until golden brown on one side, then flip them and fry the other side.

Cals. per serving	Carbs	Fat	Protein
167	16g	7g	10g

Herb Scramble

Serves 2 (Serving Size: ½ cup)

INGREDIENTS:

4 large eggs

1 teaspoon extra virgin olive oil

2 fresh basil leaves, finely chopped

1 teaspoon chives, finely chopped

1 teaspoon parsley, finely chopped

1 tablespoon avocado, diced

Cals. per serving	Carbs	Fat	Protein
212	0.5g	18g	12g

RECIPE:

Break eggs into a bowl. Heat oil in a medium-sized pan over medium heat. Add eggs, and stir with spatula. Move mixture around pan until almost done. Add basil, chives, and parsley, and continue cooking to desired consistency. Transfer to a serving plate, season with salt and pepper to taste, and top with avocado.

Be present at our table, Lord. Be here and everywhere adored.

Without Thy love we'd not be fed. We thank Thee for our daily bread.

4

Multi-Grain Pancakes

Serves 8 (Serving Size: 3 pancakes, using a $1/4$ cup of batter for each pancake)

Only a couple of changes were made to this pancake recipe to save 65 calories per serving by reducing the fat and sugar content.

We replaced the whole milk with skim milk and reduced the maple syrup proportion.

Both versions of the recipe use whole wheat flour, which offers more fiber and B-vitamins than white flour. It will also slow down the release of sugar from this dish, into your bloodstream, helping regulate blood sugar. Note the use of natural apple sauce, which has no added sugar.

If possible, use organic fruit to reduce the intake of harmful pesticides.

INGREDIENTS:

2 large eggs

1 medium banana

$1\frac{1}{2}$ cups whole wheat flour

$1/3$ cup instant oatmeal

$1/3$ cup wheat germ

1 tablespoon baking powder

1 teaspoon cinnamon

2 cups skim milk

4 ounces natural applesauce

olive oil cooking spray

4 tablespoons maple syrup

RECIPE:

Combine eggs and banana and stir. Add flour, oatmeal, wheat germ, baking powder, cinnamon, milk, and applesauce. Stir everything together until it is well mixed.

Spray olive oil cooking spray onto a pan. Heat pan on stove over medium heat. Pour pancake mix by $1/4$ cups onto pan. When edges are dry and bubbles appear on top, flip the pancakes. When the pancakes are light brown on the bottom, remove from pan.

Serve warm with pure maple syrup, fresh berries, or all-fruit jam.

Cals. per serving	Carbs	Fat	Protein
215	37g	3g	10g

Zucchini Veggie Frittata

Serves 4 (Serving Size: 1½ cups)

INGREDIENTS:

½ small sweet onion, chopped

9 eggs

1 small zucchini, thinly sliced

4 tablespoons skim milk

3 button mushrooms, thinly sliced

¾ cup shredded mozzarella cheese

1 small jar roasted red peppers, sliced

salt and pepper to taste

Cals. per serving	Carbs	Fat	Protein
231.5	10g	11.5g	22g

RECIPE:

Sauté all vegetables except red peppers until lightly brown in oven-proof frying pan sprayed with cooking spray.

Beat eggs with skim milk. Add salt and pepper to taste.

Pour eggs over veggies and add red peppers.

Cook over medium heat. Lift sides with spatula to allow raw egg to run under veggies.

Put pan in a 375-degree oven to cook the top of the frittata until firm, but not over-browned.

Remove from oven, turn onto platter, and sprinkle with cheese while it is still warm.

LUNCH

Lord Christ, as we come together for our meal at
Noontime, we remember it is the time of the day
That you offered Yourself, on the Cross, in love to
Save us. Please bless this meal as we offer
Ourselves to You and Your glory.
Amen.

Sister of the Society of the Transfiguration

Barley-Apricot Salad with Roasted Hazelnuts

Serves 8 (Serving Size: 1 cup)

Whole grain barley, hazelnuts, and apricots provide a great source of fiber that can help fight cancer and help the digestive system. Using cranberry rather than orange juice provides you with antioxidants. Low-fat yogurt is a good source of protein and will be lower in sugar than flavored yogurt. Thyme has antimicrobial effects and cinnamon is an anti-inflammatory spice that offers sweetness without calories.

INGREDIENTS:

2 whole scallions, chopped
1 cup dried apricots, chopped
½ cup roasted hazelnuts, chopped
¼ cup fresh parsley, chopped
½ teaspoon cinnamon
3½ cups vegetable broth
½ cup orange or cranberry juice
2 cups barley
1 teaspoon salt
1 tablespoon olive oil
2 teaspoons honey
1 cup plain yogurt

1 teaspoon fresh thyme
½ cup raisin or berry vinegar
⅛ teaspoon fresh ground nutmeg

RECIPE:

In a large bowl, combine scallions, apricots, hazelnuts, parsley, and cinnamon, and set aside.

Mix the broth and the juice in a medium saucepan and bring to a boil. Add the salt, oil, and barley and cook according to directions on the barley package. Keeping cover on, remove from heat and allow to cool. Once cool, fold in the scallion and apricot mixture and toss.

Whisk together the honey and the yogurt, and fold in the thyme and vinegar to make a sweet dressing. Scoop the barley mixture into a large bowl, add the scallion-apricot-hazelnut mixture in the center, and pour the dressing over all. Sprinkle with fresh ground nutmeg and serve.

Cals. per serving	Carbs	Fat	Protein
244	37g	8g	6g

Pureed Vegetable Soup

Serves 6 (Serving Size: 1 1/2 cups)

INGREDIENTS:

2 tablespoons extra virgin olive oil

3 leeks, white and light-green parts,
    finely chopped

4 carrots, peeled and sliced

1 medium zucchini, sliced

1 pound potatoes, cut into small cubes

2 tablespoons tomato paste

6 cups fat-free, low-sodium chicken broth

1 (15½-ounce) can cannellini beans, rinsed
    and drained

1½ tablespoons fresh lemon juice

salt and pepper to taste

parsley, chopped for garnish (optional)

RECIPE:

In a large saucepan, over medium heat, heat the oil. Add leeks and sauté until softened. Add carrots, zucchini, and potatoes and sauté until they begin to soften. Add the broth and tomato paste, and partially cover and simmer about 30 minutes, or until vegetables are soft. Stir in the lemon juice and the cannellini beans. Remove pan from the heat.

Working in batches, puree the soup in a blender, and pour into a second sauce pan. Return the soup to the stove, and add salt and pepper to taste. Serve immediately. Garnish with parsley if desired.

Cals. per serving	Carbs	Fat	Protein
249.5	42g	5.5g	8g

Chilled Avocado Soup

Serves 4 (Serving Size: 1 cup)

This recipe is packed with healthy fats from the avocados as well as good sources of calcium in the buttermilk and yogurt. Cumin is also an anti-inflammatory, which may offer protection against heart disease and cancer.

INGREDIENTS:

2 ripe medium avocados, halved, pitted
1 cup buttermilk
½ cup plain yogurt
2 tablespoons fresh lime juice
½ tablespoon seeded jalapeño chili, chopped
½ teaspoon chili powder
½ teaspoon (or more to taste) cumin
1 cup low-sodium chicken broth
salt and pepper to taste

RECIPE:

Cut avocados in half, remove pit, and scrape avocados from their skin into a food processor. Add buttermilk and yogurt; purée until smooth. Mix in lime juice, jalapeño, chili powder, and cumin. With machine running, blend in 1 cup of broth. Season with salt and pepper. Chill soup. (Can be made 1 day ahead. Cover and keep chilled.)

Thin soup with more broth if desired. Spoon into bowls. Serve topped with chopped red onion, jalapeño, and cilantro if desired.

Cals. per serving	Carbs	Fat	Protein
210	17g	14g	4g

Edamame Salad

Serves 6 (Serving Size: 2/3 cup)

Edamame beans are a complete source of vegetarian protein, containing all the amino acids, as well as dietary fiber, omega-3 fatty acids, and micronutrients, particularly folic acid, manganese, and vitamin K.

Cals. per serving	Carbs	Fat	Protein
62.5	5g	2.5g	5g

INGREDIENTS:

1 (16-ounce) package frozen edamame, cooked according to package directions and chilled
2 boiled eggs, chopped
1/8 cup onion, chopped
2 tablespoons celery, chopped
2 tablespoons bell pepper, chopped
2 tablespoons pimento
1/4 cup fat-free mayonnaise
salt and pepper to taste

RECIPE:

Mix all ingredients together and chill.

"Nevertheless He left not Himself without witness, in that He did good, and gave us rain from heaven, and fruitful seasons, filling our hearts with food and gladness."

Acts 14:17

Fiesta Chicken Salad

Serves 4 (Serving Size: 2¼ cups)

This is a great dish that bypasses the usual mayonnaise. It instead blends mango, lime juice, salsa, and chickpeas to offer you a nutrition-packed, flavorful dish. Mango is an excellent source of vitamin A and flavonoids like beta-carotene, alpha-carotene, and beta-cryptoxan-thin, which all have antioxidant properties. Chickpeas are a good source of fiber.

Cals. per serving	Carbs	Fat	Protein
465	36g	9g	60g

INGREDIENTS:

25 ounces of chicken breast

1 (7-ounce) can of Mexican salsa verde

1 (15½-ounce) can of chickpeas, drained

1 small red onion, chopped

½ red or orange sweet bell pepper, chopped

1 fresh mango, chopped

2 cloves of garlic, finely chopped

1 tablespoon fresh thyme

1 teaspoon ground cumin

¼ teaspoon red pepper flakes

½ lime, juiced

dash of salt and pepper

RECIPE:

Combine all ingredients; let sit for a few hours, refrigerated, until serving.

L'Insalata Verde Splendida

Serves 4 (Serving Size: 3 cups)

This salad, whose name translates as "splendid green salad," is full of healthy ingredients. Whenever possible, use organic ingredients because of their lack of pesticides, herbicides, and fungicides and is more environmentally friendly.

INGREDIENTS:

¼ cup of olive oil

1 head lettuce, chopped

1 tablespoon Italian herbs

½ teaspoon ground black pepper

2 cloves garlic, crushed

2–3 celery stalks including the leaves, diced

½ green pepper, diced

1 medium onion, diced

2 teaspoons bleu cheese

3 marinated artichoke hearts, diced

1 avocado, diced

2 tomatoes cut into wedges

2 tablespoons of the marinating liquid from the artichoke container

assorted lettuces to set aside—Boston, butter crunch, red leaf Romaine, arugula, or mustard greens

RECIPE:

In a large salad bowl mix all the ingredients except for the assorted lettuces. Liquefy the bleu cheese with large spoon, crushing the cheese into the chopped ingredients until the oil base becomes milky-white.

Then, fold all into the oil-herb-cheese-vegetable-marinade mixture. Cover and refrigerate.

Just before serving, add 1 to 2 tablespoons balsamic vinegar to taste. Blend all together.

Remove the chilled leaves from head of Boston, red leaf, butter crunch, small Romaine, or some other leaf lettuce. Including some arugula or mustard greens will add a slightly bitter zest to the mix. Tear into small pieces and add to the salad bowl. Toss the salad ingredients together and serve.

Notes:

1) Other oils could be used, but extra virgin olive oil gives a richer flavor.
2) Iceberg head lettuce or large size heads of Romaine will not make as tasty a salad as leaf lettuces.
3) Mix several colors of lettuce together for beauty.
4) Experiment with mixes of other greens for variety. Try Swiss chard or spinach.
5) In wintertime, plum tomatoes usually taste better than others.

Cals. per serving	Carbs	Fat	Protein
143	14g	7.5g	3g

Grain and veggies, fruit, and meat,

Thank you, God, for all we eat.

Thank you for the hands you made

That today, this table laid.

Amen.

Joan Barnwell

Maple Mustard Salad Dressing

Serves 6 (Serving Size: 1¼ ounces)

The fusion of maple and mustard in this recipe creates a unique flavor. Enjoy on Bibb lettuce with crumbled egg and shrimp.

INGREDIENTS:

½ cup cider vinegar
¼ cup extra virgin olive oil
1 tablespoon Dijon-style mustard
1 tablespoon real Vermont maple syrup
1 teaspoon tarragon
1 teaspoon basil
salt and pepper to taste

RECIPE:

Thoroughly mix all ingredients together until well blended. Pour mixture over salad in desired amounts and toss.

Cals. per serving	Carbs	Fat	Protein
73	3g	7g	0g

"Therefore let us keep the feast, not with old leaven, neither with the leaven of malice and wickedness; but with the unleavened bread of sincerity and truth."

1 Corinthians 5:8

Marinated Vegetable Salad

Serves 6 (Serving Size: 1 1/2 cups)

When possible, you may want to use frozen vegetables in place of canned vegetables. Frozen vegetables retain more vitamins and minerals and don't contain extra sodium that you may find in canned foods. The sugar in this recipe has been replaced with Truvia, a brand of stevia which is a calorie-free, all-natural sweetener derived from a plant.

INGREDIENTS:

Salad

1 medium green pepper, chopped

1 medium onion, chopped

3 celery ribs, chopped

1 (15-ounce) can sweet peas, rinsed and drained

1 (14-ounce) can french-cut green beans, rinsed and drained

1 (11-ounce) can white shoe peg corn, drained

2 (4-ounce) jars diced pimentos, including juices

1/2 teaspoon salt

1/4 teaspoon pepper

Dressing

2 tablespoons Truvia (powder or liquid)

1 teaspoon dry mustard

1/2 cup water

1/2 cup vinegar

RECIPE:

Mix all vegetables together in a large salad bowl. For the dressing, mix Truvia, dry mustard, 1/2 cup water, and vinegar in a small sauce pan. Heat to a near boil. Remove from heat and allow to cool for 30 minutes. Gently stir dressing into vegetable mixture. Cover and chill. Serve cold or room temperature.

Keeps well in the fridge for several days

Cals. per serving	Carbs	Fat	Protein
124.5	25g	0.5g	5g

Mediterranean Wrap

Serves 4 (Serving Size: I wrap)

INGREDIENTS:

½ cup water

⅓ cup whole wheat couscous

1 cup fresh parsley, chopped

½ cup fresh mint, chopped

¼ cup lemon juice

3 tablespoons extra virgin olive oil

2 teaspoons garlic, minced

¼ teaspoon salt, divided

¼ teaspoon freshly ground pepper

1 pound chicken tenders, boneless
   and skinless

2 tomatoes, chopped

1 cup cucumber, chopped

4 (10-inch) spinach tortillas

Cals. per serving	Carbs	Fat	Protein
445	47g	15g	30.5g

RECIPE:

Bring water to a boil in a small saucepan. Stir in couscous and remove from the heat. Cover and let stand for 5 minutes. Fluff with a fork and set aside.

Combine parsley, mint, lemon juice, oil, garlic, ⅛ teaspoon salt, and pepper in a small bowl.

Toss chicken tenders in a medium bowl with 1 tablespoon of the parsley mixture and the remaining ⅛ teaspoon salt. Place the tenders in a large non-stick skillet and cook over medium heat until cooked (3 to 5 minutes on each side). Transfer to cutting board and cut into bite-size pieces when cool enough to handle.

Stir the remaining parsley mixture into the couscous, along with the tomato and cucumber.

To assemble wraps, spread about ¾ cup of the couscous mixture onto each wrap. Divide the chicken among the wraps. Roll the wraps up like a burrito, tucking in the sides to hold the ingredients in. Cut in half and serve.

Spinach Salad with Bitter Herbs

Serves 10 (Serving Size: 2 cups)

This salad is packed with at least seven healthy greens to provide a great blend of textures and flavors as well as vitamins and minerals, especially from the spinach. Romaine lettuce is the most nutrient-dense of all lettuces and is an excellent source of vitamins A, B1, B2, C, folic acid, manganese, and chromium.

Use a vinaigrette with only 3–4 ingredients and no preservatives or additives, or make your own using flavored balsamic vinegar and extra virgin olive oil.

Cals. per serving	Carbs	Fat	Protein
184	21g	8g	7g

INGREDIENTS:

1 package fresh spinach
2 endives (leaves only), chopped
1 head Boston lettuce, chopped
1 head red cabbage, shredded
1 bunch arugula
1 bunch radicchio, shredded
1 handful watercress, chopped
½ cup fresh basil, chopped
¼ cup fresh oregano, chopped
4 eggs, hard-boiled
2 cups light berry vinaigrette

RECIPE:

Wash all the greens and toss into a large salad bowl. Crumble the hard-boiled eggs over the salad, and serve with a light berry vinaigrette.

Pork Shoulder Chili

Serves: 12 (Serving Size: 1½ cups)

While this was a healthy recipe to begin with, we saved over 140 calories per serving, but more importantly, we used healthier pork that's better for the environment and us. We recommend using pork that is lean, hormone- and antibiotic-free, and grass-fed.

We also used extra virgin olive oil because of its anti-inflammatory properties; organic vegetables whenever possible; reduced sodium canned beans, which we rinsed before using; and whole grain rice without garnish. We don't think you need to add anything to this flavorful dish. To reduce sodium further, you can use dried beans.

Cals. per serving	Carbs	Fat	Protein
428	46.5g	12.5g	32.5g

INGREDIENTS:

3 tablespoons extra virgin olive oil

3 pounds pork shoulder, lean only

1 teaspoon sea salt

1 teaspoon freshly ground black pepper

2 tablespoons ancho chili powder

1 tablespoon ground cumin

1 tablespoon cayenne pepper

1 tablespoon dried oregano

2 onions, diced

10 garlic cloves, halved

3 canned chipotle peppers in adobo

1 serrano chili, chopped

1 teaspoon sugar or honey

2 tablespoons tomato paste

1 (28-ounce) can whole tomatoes, crushed by hand

1 (28-ounce) can plus 1 (14½ ounce) can dark red kidney beans, reduced sodium, rinsed

½ cup masa harina to thicken

steamed whole grain rice

RECIPE:

In a large Dutch oven, heat the olive oil. Season the pork shoulder all over with salt and pepper, add it to the pot and brown it. For a good sear, do not crowd the pan; cook in batches if necessary.

Once browned, stir in the chili powder, cumin, cayenne, and oregano with the pork. Lower the temperature under the meat to "toast" the spices, 2 to 3 minutes. In a food processor, puree the onions, garlic, chilis, peppers, tomato paste, and sugar and add mixture to the pot.

Add the tomatoes with their liquid and enough water to cover; about 2 cups (do not add the water now if using a pressure cooker). Bring to a boil and skim off any foam that rises to the surface. Reduce the heat and simmer uncovered until the meat is fork-tender and comes apart with no resistance, about 2 hours. As it cooks down, add more water if necessary.

Use a potato masher to mash the chili so the meat comes apart in shreds. When done, stir in the kidney beans and the masa harina to thicken (optional). Warm through. Serve over rice and garnish each serving with the shredded cheddar cheese, chives, or green onions and/or sour cream (optional).

Pressure Cooker Option: Once chili is prepped, before adding the water, transfer it to a 6-quart pressure cooker and cook for 18 minutes on high pressure with natural release. Transfer the finished chili back into the Dutch oven and mash the pork. Add the water, kidney beans, and masa harina (optional) and simmer for 30 minutes.

Summer Stuffed Tomato Salad

Serves 4 (Serving Size: 1 stuffed tomato)

Cool and soothing, this salad makes a great first course or light lunch. Low-fat cottage cheese is a good source of protein and calcium, and the tomatoes provide an excellent source of antioxidants, especially vitamin C and beta carotene.

INGREDIENTS:

4 medium tomatoes

2 cups low-fat cottage cheese

2 tablespoons reduced-calorie mayonnaise

2 scallions, thinly sliced

½ medium green pepper, finely chopped

1 celery rib, thinly sliced

1 tablespoon parsley, chopped

salt and freshly ground pepper to taste

RECIPE:

Core the tomatoes and cut them partially into quarters, stopping about ¼ inch from the bottom. Gently pull apart the sections to open up the center while leaving the tomato intact. Season with salt and pepper to taste.

In a medium bowl, combine the cottage cheese, mayonnaise, scallions, bell pepper, and celery.

Mound the cottage cheese mixture into the tomatoes, dividing evenly, sprinkle the parsley over the top.

Cals. per serving	Carbs	Fat	Protein
149	12.5g	5g	13.5g

Sweet Potato Soup

Serves 6 (Serving Size: 1 cup)

At only 115 calories per medium potato, sweet potatoes are a diet-conscious diner's treat—rich in vitamin A and niacin. Here, the bright, citrusy flavor of fresh orange juice enlivens the natural sweetness of the potatoes.

INGREDIENTS:

3 medium sweet potatoes (about 2 pounds), peeled and cut into 1-inch chunks

3 cups reduced-sodium chicken broth

½ cup fresh orange juice

2 tablespoons Dijon-style mustard

¼ teaspoon salt

¼ teaspoon freshly ground pepper

dash of cayenne pepper

6 teaspoons reduced-calorie sour cream

1½ teaspoons orange zest, minced

RECIPE:

Place the sweet potato chunks in a large saucepan and add the chicken broth. Bring to a boil, reduce the heat to medium, and cook partially covered, stirring occasionally, until the sweet potatoes are tender, about 20 minutes.

Working in batches if necessary, puree the soup in a blender or food processor until very smooth. Return to the saucepan and bring to a simmer over the heat. Stir in the orange juice, mustard, salt, pepper, and cayenne. Serve at once in individual bowls, garnished with 1 teaspoon of sour cream and ¼ teaspoon minced orange zest.

Cals. per serving	Carbs	Fat	Protein
76.5	15g	0.5g	3g

Wheatberry and White Bean Salad

Serves 10 (Serving Size: 1 cup)

This is a unique recipe packed with nutrition, taste, and features an unusual grain.

Wheatberries are a whole grain and are as easy to prepare as rice. They are what flour is made from. Because they are not processed they are packed with fiber, protein, and iron and they offer an earthy flavor and toothsome bite. The beans offer up even more fiber, protein, and iron.

Cals. per serving	Carbs	Fat	Protein
139	18.5g	5g	5g

INGREDIENTS:

1 cup wheatberries

4 cups water

2 (15½-ounce) cans cannellini beans, rinsed and drained

½ cup fresh chives, chopped

½ cup zucchini or yellow squash, chopped

½ cup plum tomatoes, diced

¼ cup fresh basil, chopped

fresh spinach and variegated arugula (leaves of multiple colors)

Vinaigrette

¼ cup extra virgin olive oil

2 tablespoons Dijon-style mustard

3 garlic cloves, pressed

1 cup apple cider vinegar

RECIPE:

In a large pot, cook the wheatberries in 2 cups of water (about 30 minutes until water is absorbed), then drain. Combine the wheatberries and beans in a large bowl, and make a cover layer with the chives, zucchini, tomatoes, and basil. *Do not mix.*

Prepare the vinaigrette as follows: In a small bowl, pour ¼ cup of extra virgin olive oil and add 1 cup of cider vinegar. Mix in 2 tablespoons of a spicy mustard (Dijon or some other), a dash of salt, and a dash of pepper. Force 3 small garlic cloves through a press and add to mixture. Beat vigorously with a fork or whisk for about 1 minute; then pour vinaigrette over the wheatberry and bean dish. Once again, *do not mix.*

Cover with plastic wrap and allow to chill for several hours. Just before serving, toss the salad and pour it out onto a large platter of fresh spinach and variegated arugula for serving.

West African Peanut Chicken Soup

Serves 6 (Serving Size: 1½ cups)

We made a couple of modifications to the recipe as originally submitted, and added brown rice, which offers more fiber and slows down the release of sugar into the bloodstream; skinless chicken breasts, which have fewer saturated fats; all-natural peanut butter with no added sugar; and substituted extra virgin olive oil for regular olive oil because it has higher omega-3 levels.

INGREDIENTS:

1 pound skinless chicken breast, chopped

2 medium onions, chopped

2 large red or green peppers, chopped

2 tablespoon extra virgin olive oil

3 cloves garlic, mashed

1 (28-ounce) can tomatoes, coarsely chopped

8 cups fat-free, low-sodium chicken stock (saved from boiling chicken)

¼ teaspoon black pepper

¼ teaspoon crushed red pepper flakes

½ cup brown rice

⅔ cup peanut butter (all natural, no sugar added)

RECIPE:

You will need cooked chicken for this recipe. Simmer chicken pieces for 30 to 45 minutes. The broth can then be used in the recipe.

In a large pot, sauté onion, peppers, and garlic in oil over medium heat until onions begin to brown.

Add other ingredients except rice, chicken, and peanut butter. Simmer uncovered for 1 hour.

Add rice and chicken; simmer for 15 minutes or until rice is tender. Add peanut butter and mix until completely dissolved and smooth.

Heat to a simmer and serve.

Cals. per serving	Carbs	Fat	Protein
457	35g	21g	32g

White Chili

Serves 12 (Serving Size: 1⅓ cups)

INGREDIENTS:

12 ounces dried Great Northern Beans

2 pounds boneless chicken breasts

1 tablespoon extra virgin olive oil

2 onions, chopped

4 cloves garlic, minced

8 ounces canned diced mild green chilies

6 cups chicken stock (fat-free, low-sodium)

2 teaspoons ground cumin

1½ teaspoons dried oregano

¼ teaspoon cayenne pepper

1 cup fat-free Monterey Jack cheese

salt and pepper to taste

RECIPE:

Note: This recipe can be made with canned beans rather than dried, and can be made ahead and reheated. If you desire a thicker chili, remove some liquid from the pan and mix it with flour before adding back to the pan.

Rinse beans (pick out discolored ones), then place in a large pot and add enough cold water to cover by at least 3 inches. Soak overnight according to the instructions on the package of beans.

Place chicken in large saucepan; add cold water to cover chicken and bring to a simmer. Cook just until tender, about 15 minutes. Drain and cool, then cut into cubes. Drain beans.

Heat oil in large pot over medium-high heat. Add onions and sauté until translucent, about 10 minutes. Stir in garlic, chilies, cumin, oregano, and cayenne pepper and sauté for 2 minutes. Add beans and chicken stock and bring to a boil. Reduce heat and simmer (covered) until beans are very tender, about 2 hours.

Add chicken cubes and 1 cup Monterey Jack cheese and stir until cheese is completely melted. Season to taste with salt and pepper. Ladle into bowls. Can be served with extra cheese sprinkled on top, along with a dollop of sour cream and chopped fresh cilantro.

Cals. per serving	Carbs	Fat	Protein
249	16.5g	10g	34.5g

APPETIZERS

Recipe for Living

2 heaping cups of Patience

1 heartful of Love

2 handfuls of Generosity

1 headful of Understanding

A dash of Laughter

Sprinkle generously with Kindness and plenty
of Faith. Mix well. Spread over a lifetime, and
serve to everyone you meet.

Marilyn Morrow

Brie Crisps

Serves 8 (Serving Size: 4½ crisps)

This recipe allows for a balance of indulgence and nutrition. Brie is a good source of calcium. Butter adds 15 grams of fat to this recipe, so we counterbalanced it by adding whole wheat flour for more vitamins and minerals. Enjoy in moderation.

INGREDIENTS:

4 ounces ripe brie at room temperature

½ cup butter at room temperature

⅔ cup whole wheat flour

2 generous dashes ground cayenne pepper

⅛ teaspoon salt

⅛ teaspoon paprika

RECIPE:

Combine cheese and butter in food processor until creamy. Add flour, cayenne pepper, and salt. Pulse in processor until dough forms a ball.

Turn dough onto plastic wrap. Make into a cylinder, 2 inches in diameter. Wrap dough tightly. Refrigerate 30 minutes or overnight if desired.

Preheat oven to 400 degrees. Slice dough into ¼ inch rounds. Place on baking sheet about 2 inches apart. Bake until brown, about 10–12 minutes. Cool on rack. Sprinkle with paprika.

Cals. per serving	Carbs	Fat	Protein
153	4g	15g	0.5g

Holy Hummus

Serves 12 (Serving Size: ⅓ cup)

The primary ingredient (chickpeas or garbanzo beans) is a great source of fiber, which supports a healthy digestive system and promotes regularity. Tahini is a paste made from sesame seeds, which are a good source of manganese, copper, calcium, magnesium, iron, phosphorus, vitamin B1, zinc, and dietary fiber.

INGREDIENTS:

½ medium sweet onion
1 (16-ounce) can chick peas, drained
1 cup tahini
⅓ cup lemon juice
1 (4-ounce) jar sweet roasted peppers
1 tablespoon Tabasco sauce
1 tablespoon salt

RECIPE:

Using a food processor, chop onion and add the chick peas. Begin blending and add tahini. Add lemon juice and continue to mix until ingredients are blended.

Add roasted peppers and salt. Blend again. Add Tabasco sauce to taste.

Place in container and refrigerate overnight. Serve with toasted pita wedges.

Cals. per serving	Carbs	Fat	Protein
96	7.5g	6g	3g

Kosher Dill Pickles

Serves 60 (Serving Size: 1 spear)

A great idea for a low-calorie appetizer which also satisfies that desire to eat something crunchy. These are salty, so eat sparingly if you're concerned about high-sodium foods.

INGREDIENTS:

15 small pickling cucumbers, washed very well

40 fresh dill sprigs or 2 tablespoons dried dill weed

2 large onions, thinly sliced

5 cloves garlic, sliced

1 quart water

1 quart white vinegar

¾ cup kosher salt

RECIPE:

Cut each cucumber lengthwise into four spears. In a large bowl, combine the cucumbers, dill, onions, and garlic; set aside.

In a Dutch oven, combine the remaining ingredients. Bring to a boil; cook and stir just until salt is dissolved. Pour over cucumber mixture and gently mix; cool slightly.

Place pickles in a 1 gallon jar, cover, and refrigerate.

Pickles are ready to serve in 24 hours, and will keep in the refrigerator for 6 to 8 months.

Cals. per serving	Carbs	Fat	Protein
4	1g	0g	0g

Nana Queen's Sugared Pecans

Serves 8 (Serving Size: 2 ounces)

The pecans make this dish nutritious by providing a cholesterol-lowering benefit along with fiber, antioxidants, and vitamin C. Cinnamon has anti-inflammatory properties as well.

INGREDIENTS:

1 pound shelled pecans
¾ cup raw sugar
1 egg white
1 tablespoon salt
1 tablespoon water
1 tablespoon cinnamon

RECIPE:

Preheat oven to 200 degrees. Spray cookie sheet with non-stick spray.

Beat egg white and water until the mixture is frothy. Stir in pecans.

In separate bowl or cup, mix sugar, cinnamon, and salt together. Pour sugar mixture over pecans to coat.

Spread pecans evenly on prepared cookie sheet. Bake 1 hour until crunchy.

Cool and divide into portions.

Cals. per serving	Carbs	Fat	Protein
275	22.5g	19g	3.5g

SIDE DISHES

Lord, bless the hands which grew the wheat.

Lord, bless the hands which milked the cow.

Lord, bless the hands which butchered the meat.

Lord, bless the food before us now.

Lord, bless the one who filled the cup.

Lord, bless the one who set the place.

Lord, bless those with whom we sup.

Lord, bless us who now say grace.

Lord, bless the one who is alone.

Lord, bless the one whose table's bare.

Lord, bless the ones to us unknown.

Lord, bless all those who are not here.

Alexandra Zepeda

Roasted Asparagus

Serves 4 (Serving Size: 5 to 6 spears)

INGREDIENTS:

½ **pound fresh asparagus spears, washed and with the ends cut off**

1 teaspoon extra virgin olive oil

fresh ground salt and pepper to taste

1 tablespoon shredded parmesan cheese

Cals. per serving	Carbs	Fat	Protein
21.5	1g	1.5g	1g

RECIPE:

Preheat oven to 425 degrees.

Place aluminum foil on a baking sheet. Drizzle olive oil on the foil.

Place asparagus spears on the foil and roll them around in the oil. Freshly grind salt and pepper on the spears.

Roast in a 425-degree oven for about 5 minutes. Check for desired doneness.

Remove from baking sheet with tongs onto a serving plate in a single layer. Sprinkle them with Parmesan cheese.

To God who gives our daily bread, a thankful song we raise, and pray
that He who sends us food, may fill our hearts with praise.

Southern Caviar
(Bean Salsa with Black-eyed Peas)

Serves 8 (Serving Size: 3/4 cup)

Black-eyed peas are beans that provide a good source of fiber and potassium to help regulate blood pressure. Tomatoes are a good source of lycopene, which can fight some diseases, including prostate cancer, and green bell peppers offer carotenoids, which are antioxidants, and calcium.

INGREDIENTS:

3 Roma tomatoes, chopped

1 green bell pepper, chopped

6 green onions, white part only, chopped

1 (10-ounce) can Rotel tomatoes w/chilies, hot or original

1 (16-ounce) can black-eyed peas, drained and rinsed

1 (7-ounce) can shoepeg corn

8 ounces zesty fat-free Italian dressing

RECIPE:

Put chopped ingredients in a glass container and cover with several tablespoons of the Rotel tomatoes.

Add the rest of the ingredients and pour remaining Rotel tomatoes and Italian dressing on top.

Cover and chill overnight. Stir after 12 hours.

Serve with chips.

Cals. per serving	Carbs	Fat	Protein
106.5	22g	0.5g	3.5g

Chilled Dilled Peas

Serves 4 (Serving Size: 1 cup)

This recipe was modified by using fat-free sour cream, which cuts out all the fat while leaving in the calcium and protein. The curry powder has anti-inflammatory properties, as well.

This recipe doubles well and is inexpensive to make.

INGREDIENTS:

1 teaspoon curry powder (or to taste)

1 cup fat-free sour cream

½ cup fresh snipped chives

¼ cup fresh snipped dill

1 (16-ounce) can tiny peas, drained and rinsed in cold water or 1 (10-ounce) box frozen peas, cooked, drained, and chilled

RECIPE:

Combine curry powder, sour cream, chives, and dill; add peas and mix gently but thoroughly.

Garnish with additional fresh dill and chill. This makes an excellent first course, vegetable dish, or appetizer.

Cals. per serving	Carbs	Fat	Protein
112	21g	0g	7g

Cinnamon-Baked Squash

Serves 4 (Serving Size: 1 cup)

We made one healthy change which kept the calorie counts the same, but increased the heart-health benefit by substituting olive oil for the butter. The cinnamon has great anti-inflammatory properties and adds sweetness without adding calories. Note: Sweet spice adds a piquant touch to yellow squash and cost nothing in added fat or calories. This dish goes especially well with most pork dishes.

INGREDIENTS:

3 medium yellow squash

1 tablespoon olive oil

½ teaspoon cinnamon

¼ teaspoon salt

¼ teaspoon freshly ground pepper

RECIPE:

Preheat the oven to 350 degrees.

Scrub squash well and pat dry. Trim and cut crosswise on the diagonal into ¼-inch slices.

Arrange the slices of squash in a single layer on a large non-stick baking sheet. Brush lightly with oil and sprinkle the cinnamon evenly. Season with salt and pepper.

Bake 8 to 10 minutes, or until the squash is tender. Serve hot.

Cals. per serving	Carbs	Fat	Protein
55	5g	3g	2g

Dhal Rice Pilaf

Serves 4 (Serving Size: ³/₄ cup)

This dish comes from Sri Lanka. At first glance, it seems to contain a lot of carbohydrates, but they come in the form of rice and beans, which makes this dish an excellent source of complete protein–perfect for vegetarians. We used whole grain basmati rice since it has most of the fiber and much of the vitamins and minerals found in whole grain.

INGREDIENTS:

1 cup red lentils

½ cup wild rice

½ cup whole grain basmati rice

2 teaspoons sesame seeds

1 medium onion, sliced

1 small stick cinnamon

2–4 whole dried red chilies (depending on how spicy you like it)

2 tablespoons extra virgin olive oil

8 curry leaves (optional)

pinch turmeric powder

⅛ cup toasted cashew nuts, roughly chopped

salt to taste

RECIPE:

Wash and cook the wild and basmati rice in 2 cups of water. When rice is just cooked and all the water has evaporated, take off the heat and let it cool.

In a separate pan, cook the red lentils in 2 cups of water until they're just done. The grains should separate easily. Be careful not to overcook them as they will become a mushy mess!

In a wok or sauté pan, heat the olive oil and add the sesame seeds. The seeds will start popping. Wait 1 minute and add the onions, dried chilies, cinnamon, and curry leaves and sauté for 5 minutes. Season with salt. Add the cooked dhal and turmeric and sauté for 3 minutes. Lastly, mix in the cooked rice and the toasted cashews. Make sure the grains of rice are separate so that there are no lumps. Mix and cook for another 3 minutes. Enjoy!

Cals. per serving	Carbs	Fat	Protein
373.5	59g	9.5g	13g

Mediterranean Eggplant

Serves 4 (Serving Size: ¼ cups)

A lot of folks are familiar with baba ghanoush, which is made in Turkey with cut-up and cubed eggplants. The name *Baba* means "father" in Turkish, and in the regions where the Arab population is large, this dish can also be known as abu-ganoush, and is made with mashed, rather than cut-up, cubed eggplant.

INGREDIENTS:

1 medium eggplant (about one pound)

2 tablespoons tahini (if you don't have tahini on hand, chunky peanut butter can be used)

1 large garlic clove, crushed

2–3 teaspoons hot sesame oil

1 teaspoon coarse kosher salt

RECIPE:

Place the eggplant directly on the stove burner and roast over very low flame, turning often. You could also place it in a 375-degree oven. Roast until skin has a charred look and the eggplant collapses. Remove from heat and cool. Scoop out eggplant pulp and transfer to a small bowl. Mash until smooth and combine with remaining ingredients by hand. Can be used as a vegetable side dish, sandwich filling for pita, or a dip.

Cals. per serving	Carbs	Fat	Protein
81	7g	5g	2g

Picnic Salad

Serves 4 (Serving Size: 1¾ cups)

This salad makes an excellent, low-carb substitute for potato salad.

INGREDIENTS:

1 head cauliflower, cut or broken into
    small pieces

3 hard boiled eggs, whites only, chopped

¼ cup sweet onion, chopped

⅛ cup dill pickles, chopped

¼ cup light sour cream

¼ cup fat-free mayonnaise

2 tablespoons chopped pimento

1 teaspoon salt

1 teaspoon pepper

RECIPE:

Cook cauliflower in boiling salted water 6 to 8 minutes until soft, but not mushy. Drain and cool. It can be left in pieces or mashed, whichever you prefer. Add the other ingredients and mix well. Chill.

Cals. per serving	Carbs	Fat	Protein
109.5	15g	1.5g	9g

Roasted Cauliflower

Serves 4 (Serving Size: ³⁄₄ cup)

This recipe provides great taste as well as cauliflower's anti-inflammatory and antioxidant properties. It's also low in fat and calories. Garlic, a sulfur-containing compound, can help dilate blood vessels and help keep blood pressure under control.

The extra fat in this dish comes from the pine nuts, which offer vitamin E, an antioxidant that fights free radicals and increases immunity. To save 115 calories from the total recipe, you can leave them out.

INGREDIENTS:

½ head cauliflower
1 tablespoon extra virginolive oil
garlic cloves, peeled (as many as you like)
2 tablespoons pine nuts
salt and pepper

RECIPE:

Separate or cut cauliflower into bite-sized pieces. Rinse and dry on paper towels. Place in a large bowl. Add garlic and pine nuts. Add oil and stir to coat. Sprinkle with salt and pepper.

Place on baking sheet and bake at 400 degrees for about 30 minutes, turning 3 or 4 times. Remove from oven and serve immediately.

Cals. per serving	Carbs	Fat	Protein
195	5.5g	17g	5g

Solomon's Rainbow of Vegetables

Serves 8 (Serving Size: 1 1/2 cups)

This delicious dish is packed with vegetables of every color of the rainbow, which is a helpful guide for choosing healthy foods. The more colors we eat, the better, when it comes to fruit and vegetables. Let the rainbow be your guide.

The beans included are also a great source of fiber, low-fat and low-calorie, and when served with rice, become a great vegetarian protein source. Chili pepper also has anti-inflammatory properties that may protect the heart and fight cancer and disease. The hotter the pepper, the more capsaicin, which gives peppers their heat and anti-inflammatory properties. We only made one change—substituting the white rice with brown.

INGREDIENTS:

5 summer squash, diced

2 stalks celery, chopped

8 plum tomatoes, chopped

1 package frozen lima beans or 1 can fava beans

1 red onion, minced

1 orange pepper, chopped

1 cup pomegranate juice

2 cloves garlic, pressed

1 teaspoon salt

1/2 teaspoon chili pepper

3 cups brown rice, cooked

handful of fresh chervil or cicely (myrrh)

RECIPE:

Preheat oven to 375 degrees.

Combine all vegetables into a large bowl and toss. Pour pomegranate juice into a glass and press garlic into it; stir with a fork until well mixed. Grease a large baking pan and arrange vegetables in it, creating a rainbow of colors. Pour pomegranate/garlic juice over vegetables; add salt and pepper. Bake for 35 to 40 minutes. Remove from oven; pour into a large bowl and mix with rice and chervil. Form into balls using an ice cream scoop. Serve piping hot.

Cals. per serving	Carbs	Fat	Protein
212.5	45g	0.5g	7g

Spanish Spinach

Serves 4 (Serving Size: 2/3 cup)

INGREDIENTS:

1 pound fresh spinach, washed and trimmed,
   or 1 (10-ounce) package of frozen spinach,
   defrosted, with excess moisture squeezed out

2 teaspoons extra virgin olive oil

1/4 cup pine nuts

1/4 cup golden raisins

salt to taste

RECIPE:

Sauté spinach in olive oil over medium heat until wilted. Remove from heat; add remaining ingredients and mix well. Enjoy.

Cals. per serving	Carbs	Fat	Protein
158	19g	6g	7g

Prayer for food that didn't turn out as hoped . . .

O God, may your blessing rest now on this food

In spite of the fact that it tastes not as good

As the recipe followed promised it would.

Yet we give You thanks for the food we have;

For blessings past counting, for blessing to share.

Plus we have each other in the wonder of You

And your blessings upon us O Lord, and this food.

Amen.

Sr. Diana, CT

Spicy Yellow Squash and Onion

Serves 6 (Serving Size: 2 cups)

This is a light and healthy dish. The squash offers carotenoids which are antioxidents and protect the body from diseases such as cancer. If you can tolerate the heat, the crushed red peppers offer anti-inflammatory protection.

INGREDIENTS:

1 teaspoon extra virgin olive oil

4 medium yellow squash

1 cup red onion, thinly sliced

1 clove garlic, minced

¼ teaspoon salt

¼ teaspoon crushed red pepper (optional)

fresh ground black pepper to taste

¼ cup grated Parmesan cheese

RECIPE:

Heat the oil in the skillet. Add ingredients in order given. Cook on stove top for 10 to 15 minutes, stirring constantly. Do not let it stick. Pour into baking dish. Bake for 45 minutes in a 350-degree oven. Sprinkle with Parmesan cheese. Brown under flame. Serve hot.

Cals. per serving	Carbs	Fat	Protein
95.5	11g	3.5g	5g

Urban Potato Salad

Serves 16 (Serving Size: ½ cup)

This recipe offers a delicious variation on the traditional mayonnaise potato salad.

INGREDIENTS:

5 pounds russet potatoes

2 medium red onions

2 large red bell peppers

2 large yellow bell peppers

¾ cup extra virgin olive oil

⅓ cup balsamic vinegar

½ cup coarsely chopped Italian parsley, stems removed, plus a few sprigs for garnish

1 medium sweet yellow onion

1½ teaspoon salt

½ teaspoon coarsely ground black pepper

RECIPE:

Scrub the potatoes but leave the skins on. Place them in a large pot and cover with cold water. Bring to a boil and cook covered, until potatoes can be pierced easily with a fork. Drain and spread on a tray to cool.

While the potatoes are cooling, roast the peppers on a grill, over an open flame, or under the broiler, turning frequently until they are black on all sides. Set aside to cool.

Slice the red onions into ½-inch thick wedges. Heat ¼ cup of the olive oil in a large skillet and cook the onions over medium heat until lightly browned. Remove from heat. Add the rest of the oil and the balsamic vinegar to the skillet. Stir in the salt and pepper and set aside.

Quarter and then slice the cooled potatoes into wedges, about ½-inch thick.

Dice the yellow onion.

Remove the blackened skin, stem and seeds from the peppers. Cut the peppers in half crosswise, then slice into ¼-inch wide strips.

Combine all in a large mixing bowl. Gently toss until well mixed. Serve garnished with parsley sprigs.

It is also good (and pretty) with a mixture of russet, red, and purple potatoes—but you have to vary the boiling time for each type.

Cals. per serving	Carbs	Fat	Protein
228	30.5g	10g	3.5g

DINNER

We give thanks, O God for the food you have
given us and for the hands that prepared it.
We remember those who are hungry and alone
and pray they may know your presence and feel
your love. We ask your guidance in leading us
to those whom you would have us serve.

Barb Hagen

Baked Fish with Spinach

Serves 2 (Serving Size: 1 fillet and half the vegetables/spinach)

INGREDIENTS:

2 firm white fish fillets, 8 ounces each
    (halibut, rock fish, or tilapia)

1 (5-ounce) bag baby spinach

1 teaspoon kosher salt

1 teaspoon fresh ground pepper

Creole seasoning blend*

2 tablespoons chicken broth, fat free,
    reduced sodium

1 small tomato, chopped

2 green onions, thinly sliced

lemon juice, ½ lemon yield

1 tablespoon extra virgin olive oil

½ lemon sliced

*Or substitute a combination of sweet paprika and cayenne—1 tablespoon paprika, ¼ tablespoon cayenne, and ¼ teaspoon or so of dried thyme.

RECIPE:

Sauté the spinach in chicken broth until barely wilted. Lightly oil a baking dish large enough to hold the spinach and fish. Add the spinach and sprinkle with salt and pepper.

Season the fish to taste with salt, pepper, and Creole seasoning.

Arrange fillets over the spinach and scatter tomatoes and green onion over them.

Cover with foil and bake at 360 degrees until fish flakes with a fork, about 20 minutes.

Squeeze ½ small lemon over dish before serving.

Cals. per serving	Carbs	Fat	Protein
472	17g	16g	65g

Baked Salmon à la Nancy

Serves 6 (Serving Size: one 5⅓-ounce fillet)

This is a simple, but very healthy salmon dish. It is naturally low in carbohydrates.

INGREDIENTS:

2 pounds fresh salmon fillets
juice of 2 lemons
3 heaping tablespoons Dijon-style mustard
¼ teaspoon extra virgin olive oil

RECIPE:

Preheat oven to 375 degrees.

Use a rectangular baking dish that is large enough to hold all the fish pieces without their overlapping. Line the baking dish with foil.

Grease the foil lightly with the olive oil.

Rinse each fish fillet in cold water and pat dry. Place in baking dish skin side down.

Mix together the lemon juice and mustard until smooth. Spoon it over the fish, covering the surfaces of the pieces.

Bake uncovered for around 15 to 17 minutes or until cooked through. Do not overcook.

Remove with spatula onto a plate, gently lifting the fish off the skin (which will stick to the foil and should be left there), and serve.

Serve as is, or garnish with one or more of the following for a "dressier" look: thin lemon slices, chopped tomato, chopped parsley, capers.

You can also cut the cooked fish into individual serving-size pieces, wrap in foil, and freeze when cool. (This recipe freezes very well.)

To defrost, unwrap as many portions as you need, place on microwaveable dish, cover loosely with paper towel, and microwave for about 1½ minutes or so (depending on size) until warmed through. (Note: frozen cooked fish is best consumed within 2 weeks.)

Cals. per serving	Carbs	Fat	Protein
333	1.5g	21g	34.5g

Barbecued Tofu

Serves 4 (Serving Size: 1 cup)

Soy is a good source of polyunsaturated fats, fiber, vitamins, and minerals, as well as non-animal protein and has a low saturated fat content. It can also help lower LDL cholesterol. Ginger is an anti-inflammatory food and adds great flavor.

INGREDIENTS:

1 pound tofu
flour for dredging
2 tablespoons extra virgin olive oil
1 cup salsa
¼ cup low-sodium soy sauce
¼ cup honey
2 teaspoons minced fresh ginger root

RECIPE:

Slice tofu into ¼-inch thick pieces. Roll tofu in flour and sauté in oil until little brown on each side.

Combine salsa, soy sauce, honey, and ginger to make sauce. Cover bottom of a casserole dish with a little of the sauce, add a layer of tofu, then cover with more sauce, alternating and ending with sauce on top. Bake at 350 for 45 minutes or until bubbling.

Cals. per serving	Carbs	Fat	Protein
378	41.5g	18g	12.5g

DINNER

Chicken and White Bean Stew

Serves 16 (Serving Size: 1¼ cups)

This is a very hearty stew that is packed with protein, vitamins, and minerals.

INGREDIENTS:

2–3 tablespoons of extra virigin olive oil

2 stalks celery, finely chopped

1 carrot, peeled and finely chopped

1 small onion, finely chopped

4 stalks celery, cut into bite-size pieces

4 carrots, peeled and cut into bite-size pieces

1 bag pearl onions (fresh or frozen)

1 box button mushrooms, halved

salt and freshly ground black pepper to taste

1 tablespoon Italian seasoning

1 large bay leaf

1 (28-ounce) can whole peeled tomatoes

2 (15-ounce) cans cannellini beans, rinsed

1 box chicken stock, low sodium

1 whole chicken, cut into 8 pieces

6 hot Italian sausages (turkey)

½ pound shrimp (30–40 shrimp), peeled and deveined

1 loaf crusty bread

RECIPE:

Heat the oil in a heavy 5½-quart saucepan or Dutch oven over medium-high heat. Salt and pepper chicken pieces and brown on both sides in the oil. Set aside. Brown sausages whole and set aside.

Add the finely chopped celery, carrot, and onion. Salt and pepper the vegetables and sauté until the onion is translucent, about 10 minutes. Add the Italian seasoning and bay leaf into the vegetables. Stir in the tomatoes with their juices, chicken stock, and pieces of carrot and celery. Add the chicken pieces and sausages and press to submerge.

Bring the cooking liquid to a simmer. Reduce the heat to medium-low and simmer gently, uncovered, until the chicken is almost cooked through, stirring the mixture occasionally, about 35 minutes.

Using tongs, transfer the chicken pieces and sausage to a plate and cool for 10 minutes. Discard the bay leaf. Add the beans, pearl onions, and mushroom pieces to the pot and simmer until the liquid has reduced into a stew consistency, about 15 minutes.

Discard the skin and bones from the chicken. Shred the chicken and cut the sausage into bite-size pieces. Return the chicken meat and sausage to the stew and add the shrimp. Bring the stew just to a simmer. Ladle the stew into serving bowls and serve with the bread.

Cals. per serving	Carbs	Fat	Protein
287	32g	7g	24g

"He that is of a merry heart hath a continual feast."

Proverbs 15:15

Chicken Breast with Bourbon and Pecans

Serves 4 (Serving Size: 1 chicken breast)

This is a fast and flavorful chicken dish that's low in carbs and high in flavor. One secret tip when cooking with alcohol: use what you like to drink and stay away from so-called "cooking wines," which have high sodium levels and taste mediocre. The pecans in this dish are a good source of the anitoxidant vitamin E that fights cancer, and they are high in protein, fiber, and plant sterols, and is a natural LDL cholesterol reducer.

INGREDIENTS:

4 skinless, boneless chicken breast halves,
    4–6 ounces each
½ teaspoon salt
¼ teaspoon freshly ground pepper
1½ teaspoons butter
1½ teaspoons extra virgin olive oil
¼ cup bourbon
½ cup reduced sodium chicken broth
1½ tablespoons chopped pecans

RECIPE:

Season the chicken with salt and pepper. In a large non-stick skillet, melt the butter in the oil over medium heat. Add the chicken and cook, turning once, until lightly browned, about 5 minutes.

Transfer to a plate and cover with foil to keep warm.

Pour off any fat left in the skillet. Remove skillet from heat and pour in the bourbon. Return the skillet to high heat and bring to a boil.

Pour in the broth, return to a boil, and add chicken. Reduce heat to low, partially cover and cook, turning occasionally, 3 minutes longer.

Serve hot, spooning the pan juices over the chicken. Garnish with chopped pecans. Serve with baked acorn squash or pureed sweet potato. Note: bourbon gives a fine flavor to this simple chicken dish. Be careful when adding bourbon to a hot skillet: it can go up in flames if not poured in off the heat.

Cals. per serving	Carbs	Fat	Protein
304	1.5g	14g	43g

Chicken Enchiladas

Serves 6 (Serving Size: 2 enchiladas)

INGREDIENTS:

1 dozen fat-free whole wheat flour tortillas

1 cup fat-free sour cream

1 can Cream of Chicken soup (Campbells 98% fat-free)

1 (4-ounce) can mild chilies, chopped

3 cups cooked chicken, chopped

¾ cup fat-free sharp cheddar cheese

Cals. per serving	Carbs	Fat	Protein
354.5	43.5g	4.5g	35g

RECIPE:

Warm tortillas in oven by placing on a baking sheet, covering with moist dish towel. Heat at 250 degrees for 10 minutes.

Combine sour cream, soup, and chilies, set aside. Spread ¼ cup chicken in middle of tortilla, sprinkle on about 1 tablespoon cheese, roll tortillas and place in a 9 x 13 inch baking dish.

When all the tortillas have been filled and rolled, pour the mixture over all the tortillas. Sprinkle with remaining cheese. Bake uncovered at 350 degrees for 20 minutes or until hot, but not bubbling.

This freezes very well. Just reheat in the oven or microwave.

DINNER

Chicken, Broccoli, and Mushrooms with Tomato Sauce

Serves 4 (Serving Size: 2 cups)

INGREDIENTS:

olive oil cooking spray

1 teaspoon garlic, crushed

1 small onion (white or red), chopped

1 pound chicken breasts, cut into cubes

1 head broccoli, chopped into bite-sized pieces

12 ounces white mushrooms, sliced

1 (26-ounce) jar tomato sauce

red pepper flakes (optional)

Cals. per serving	Carbs	Fat	Protein
283	26g	7g	29g

RECIPE:

Spray a large pan with olive oil cooking spray. Over medium heat, add garlic and onion and cook for about 1 minute. Add chicken and cook until no longer pink, about 5 minutes.

Add broccoli. Cover pan and let cook about 4 minutes.

Add mushrooms and stir.

Add tomato sauce and reduce flame to low. Sprinkle with red pepper flakes to taste (if you don't like spicier food, you can omit them). Allow all ingredients to heat through. Serve immediately.

Chickenless Cacciatore

Serves 4 (Serving Size: 1 1/2 cups)

INGREDIENTS:

olive oil cooking spray

1 bag of frozen Quorn Chik'n Tenders (meat substitute)

1 small onion, chopped

1 clove garlic, chopped

1/2 pound fresh mushrooms (small portabellas are best), chopped

1 (6-ounce) can tomato paste

2 cups hot water

1/2 teaspoon thyme

1/4 teaspoon ground oregano

1/4 teaspoon allspice

1/8 teaspoon pepper

dash of sea salt

1/4 cup parsley, chopped

RECIPE:

Brown onion in just enough olive oil to prevent sticking. Combine all other ingredients except tenders and mushrooms in crockpot and stir well. Add everything else and stir again. Set crockpot on high for 20 minutes, and then on low for 3 to 4 hours.

Serve over rice or pasta.

Cals. per serving	Carbs	Fat	Protein
101	14g	1g	9g

Chicken and Mushrooms

Serves 4 (Serving Size: 2 cups)

Enjoy this well-balanced meal that's a good source of protein. Protein is an essential building block of all the body's cells, including muscles.

INGREDIENTS:

1 pound chicken breast, sliced in 2-inch pieces

1 teaspoon extra virgin olive oil

2 cans Campbell's Golden Mushroom Soup, undiluted

4 celery stalks, chopped in ½-inch pieces

4 large carrots, chopped in ½-inch pieces

⅓ medium onion, chopped

¼ pound fresh sliced mushrooms

Cals. per serving	Carbs	Fat	Protein
309	23g	9g	33g

RECIPE:

Gently sauté meat and onion in oil until about half cooked.

Add undiluted soup, carrots, and celery. Cover and cook over medium heat until carrots are just done (stir often as soup gets thicker).

Turn off heat, add mushrooms, and cover. The mushrooms will cook to the right consistency in about 5 minutes.

Serve over cooked brown rice or whole wheat pasta.

This dish is great with a green salad and French bread (bread can be omitted due to extra calories).

Easter Mussels

Serves 5 (Serving Size: 10 mussels with ½ cup sauce)

Mussels are high in healthy protein, low in fat, and an excellent source of selenium and vitamin B12, which increases metabolic processes and may help fight fatigue and depression.

INGREDIENTS:

olive oil cooking spray

½ teaspoon extra virgin olive oil

½ onion, diced

½ cup white wine or strong beer, like Guinness

2 pounds mussels

1–3 cloves garlic, minced

3–4 tomatoes, pulped

fresh ground pepper

juice of 1 lemon

Cals. per serving	Carbs	Fat	Protein
70	11g	2g	2g

RECIPE:

Spray cooking oil on heavy duty sauce pan or Dutch oven and heat over medium to medium-high flame. Cook garlic gently for a minute and add pulped tomatoes and pepper. Cook down to a paste-like consistency.

Remove from pan and add lemon juice. Whisk to be nice and liquidy. Set aside.

In the same pan as before, over medium heat, add the ½ teaspoon olive oil and sauté the onion until softened, but not transparent.

Add in the mussels and white wine or beer. Steam till open. (Extra liquid may be added if needed. The bottom of the pan should be covered in liquid, but it does not need to be deep.)

Remove mussels to serving platter. Discard any that are still tightly closed.

Add tomato mixture to remaining wine or beer in pan. Reduce to desired consistency to make sauce. This also boils off the alcohol flavor. Spoon over mussels on the platter.

Serve with crusty bread. If you use more mussels, you might want to double the sauce.

Eggplant Parmesan

Serves 6 (Serving Size: 1 cup)

This recipe is best prepared over two days, as the flavors are enhanced by overnight chilling. If you have the time, it is well worth it.

The deep purple eggplant offers many vitamins and minerals, as well as phytonutrients, which have antioxidants. The cheese is a good source of calcium.

INGREDIENTS:

Sauce:

2–3 cups dry parsley flakes (if using fresh parsley, 1–2 full heads, finely chopped)

1 large (28-ounce) can diced or crushed tomatoes

1 cup chicken broth

2 tablespoons basil

4 cloves garlic

1 teaspoon Italian seasoning

1 large (12-ounce) can tomato paste

1 large (29-ounce) can tomato sauce

1 teaspoon olive oil

Eggplant:

2 tablespoons olive oil

1 large eggplant or 2 medium eggplants

3 eggs

½ cup skim or 2% milk

Italian bread crumbs

Parmesan cheese, block, not grated

RECIPE:

Important: this is really a two day enterprise so plan accordingly.

Day 1: Sauce

Put all the sauce ingredients in a deep pan and mix well. Heat to a boil, and when bubbles rise, turn down heat to a simmer.

You will want to simmer this for about 4 to 6 hours. Stir often to ensure there is no burning. Because of the great amount of parsley, there should be a green tint to the sauce. If not, add more. The parsley will help thicken the sauce. Simmer uncovered, but if you think it is getting too thick, cover to retain moisture. If it gets too thick, add more stock. The sauce should be thick, but not pasty.

When the sauce is done, set it aside to cool. When completely cooled, keep in the refrigerator overnight.

Day 2: Eggplant

Take out the sauce and return to stove. Simmer for about 90 minutes to 2 hours. Make sure it stays moist, but not too runny. The overnight cooling is important in order to blend the flavors. *This is essential.*

Peel the eggplant. Cut into 1 inch steaks (lay eggplant on side and cut the steaks across the vegetable).

Mix the eggs and milk. Place each steak in the egg wash, and then roll them in the bread crumbs. A second wash may be needed. Make sure you have a nice crust on the eggplant.

Brown the eggplant in a skillet, using olive oil to fry it. Do not overcook.

Place the steaks in a baking pan. Spoon the sauce over the eggplant and place in a 300-degree oven. The cheese should be sliced thinly and placed on each steak during the last 5 minutes of baking. Total baking time is about 20 minutes.

Serve one steak per diner, with a tossed salad on the side. Extra sauce may be brought to the table.

Cals. per serving	Carbs	Fat	Protein
251.5	31.5g	7.5g	14.5g

Feta Shrimp

Serves 4 (Serving Size: four 1 1/4 cups)

INGREDIENTS:

1 pound jumbo shrimp or prawns
  (15–18 per pound)

4 ripe tomatoes, peeled and chopped
  (or 1 (14-ounce) can chopped tomatoes)

1 tablespoon extra virgin olive oil

1–2 cloves garlic, chopped

1/4 cup white wine

4 ounces feta, crumbled

Cals. per serving	Carbs	Fat	Protein
232.5	8g	8g	28g

RECIPE:

Simmer the tomatoes with the garlic for 20 to 30 minutes, until saucy.

Sauté the shrimp in 1 tablespoon of oil for 1 to 2 minutes.

Add the wine and tomatoes to the shrimp and cook 5 minutes or until shrimp is done.

Stir in the feta until well blended into the sauce.

Sprinkle with fresh chopped basil or parsley and can be served with brown rice.

Halibut with Tomato-Corn Salsa

Serves 2 (Serving Size: one 4-ounce fillet with 1½ cups salsa)

Halibut contains the trace mineral Selenium which helps make antioxidant enzymes that are believed to fight chronic diseases such as cancer and heart disease. Although halibut is a lean fish with a mild, sweet flavor, it does contain the important omega-3 fatty acids that protect the heart. In addition to the salsa serving as a delicious topping, it's packed with cancer-fighting properties from the tomatoes, anti-inflammatory properties from the cinnamon and garlic, and fiber from the corn.

INGREDIENTS:

2 diced plum or other type of tomato

1 onion (red or yellow), diced

1 cup frozen cut corn

1 tablespoon parsley

2 tablespoons basil leaves

1 ounce cilantro

3 tablespoons extra virgin olive oil, divided

1 teaspoon salt

1 teaspoon fresh ground pepper

1 teaspoon garlic powder

1 tablespoon lemon juice

2 halibut fillets, ½–¾ inch thick, rinsed and patted dry

RECIPE:

Place corn in a bowl (without water) and micro-wave for about 1 to 2 minutes. Drain any excess water from bowl. Add the tomatoes, onions, herbs, and spices. Add two tablespoons of olive oil. Adjust to taste.

Heat skillet with remaining one tablespoon extra virgin olive oil. Pat halibut dry and place in pan and sauté over medium heat. You may want to dust with a Cajun or blackening spice. Cook until golden brown. Place halibut on the plate, drizzle lemon juice over fish, and spoon salsa over top.

Cals. per serving	Carbs	Fat	Protein
255	37g	1g	24.5g

65

Salmon with Basil Pesto and Spinach Salad

Serves 2 (Serving Size: 1 fillet and half the salad)

We loved this dish for its simplicity and healthy ingredients. The only change we made was substituting in brown rice. Whole grain foods like brown rice offer more nutritional value as well as fiber, which helps slowly release sugar into the bloodstream, giving us more sustained energy and more time to burn the sugar with physical activity.

We also recommend using wild salmon whenever possible because of its higher levels of omega-3 fatty acids, which help fight cancer and heart disease.

INGREDIENTS:

2 (4-ounce) salmon fillets
    (preferably wild salmon)
1 cup cooked brown rice
2 cups fresh spinach
2 tomatoes
1 handful fresh basil
2 tablespoons balsamic vinegar

RECIPE:

Basil Pesto

Wash spinach and basil, chop, and place in bowl. Wash tomatoes, and cut into small pieces. Sprinkle with balsamic vinegar.

Preheat oven to 350 degrees. Place salmon in a small oven-proof pan lined with aluminum foil. Spread 1 tablespoon of basil pesto over top of each fillet, and bake for 20 to 25 minutes. Can be served over a bed of rice.

Cals. per serving	Carbs	Fat	Protein
424	40g	16g	30g

Shrimp with Onions and Peppers

Serves 4 (Serving Size: 1 cup rice and 1 cup shrimp; divide shrimp and rice into equal portions)

This is another great dish for its simplicity and healthy ingredients, including shrimp, a good source of protein, and brown rice, a good source of fiber. Some studies have shown that women who eat whole grains like brown rice, weigh less and have lower rates of cancer than women who don't.

INGREDIENTS:

1 tablespoon extra virgin olive oil
1 small onion, chopped
1 large green pepper, chopped
16 large shrimp, cleaned and shelled
juice of ½ lime
1 teaspoon Old Bay seasoning
1 cup cooked brown rice

RECIPE:

Heat the olive oil in a small skillet and add the onions and peppers. Cook on medium-high heat for 3 to 4 minutes, until onions take on a glossy texture. Add the shrimp, lime juice, and seasoning, and stir well. Cook for about 5 minutes, stirring constantly so that it does not burn. Plate on a bed of rice.

Cals. per serving	Carbs	Fat	Protein
312.5	35g	8.5g	24g

Sloppy Joes

Serves 4 (Serving Size: 1 cup)

We made some changes to this recipe, such as using grass-fed ground beef, and cutting the ketchup in half to decrease the sugar and reduce the total calories while not taking away flavor from this family favorite.

We also recommend using grass-fed ground beef when possible because it's leaner, more humanely raised, better for the environment, has more omega-3 fatty acids, and tastes great.

We also recommend serving it without the bun and substituting it with a whole grain like brown rice and vegetables.

INGREDIENTS:

1 pound 95% lean grass-fed ground beef
olive oil cooking spray
¼ cup finely chopped onion
¼ cup finely chopped green pepper
1 teaspoon yellow mustard
1 teaspoon vinegar
1 tablespoon chili powder
½ cup ketchup
3 teaspoons brown sugar
salt and pepper to taste

RECIPE:

Coat a medium skillet with olive oil cooking spray and sauté onion and peppers till translucent. Add beef and brown. Drain off liquid.

Add the rest of the ingredients and stir. Reduce heat and simmer 30 to 35 minutes. Can be served on a whole wheat bun or over brown rice.

Cals. per serving	Carbs	Fat	Protein
246	26g	6g	22g

Slumgullie

Serves 4 (Serving Size: 1 cup)

In this family recipe, we used whole wheat pasta and substituted ground turkey for the ground beef. This reduced the calories, added essential vitamins and minerals, and reduced the amount of saturated fat in this dish. You can also use ground chicken, bison, or grass-fed beef, or skip the meat and poultry to make it a vegetarian meal. If you are gluten intolerant, you can use brown rice pasta.

INGREDIENTS:

2 cups whole wheat cooked macaroni, (save the water)

fresh garlic to taste

2 tablespoons Italian seasonings (to include basil and oregano)

1 pound lean ground turkey breast

1 large onion, chopped

1 stalk celery, finely chopped

½ green pepper, finely chopped

1 large can crushed tomatoes

RECIPE:

In a large saucepan, brown ground turkey, garlic, celery, pepper, and onion until the onion is soft. Add the cooked macaroni (it should still be a little stiff), tomatoes, and Italian seasoning.

Simmer together until the liquid from the tomatoes is absorbed. If more liquid is needed, use the pasta water. Serve and enjoy.

Cals. per serving	Carbs	Fat	Protein
367	42.5g	9g	29g

Uncooked Tomato Sauce and Hot Pasta

Serves 5 (Serving Size: 1 1/2 cups)

INGREDIENTS:

2 pounds of fresh tomatoes at room
    temperature

2 or more cloves of garlic (better with 5)

1/2 cup fresh basil leaves, minced

1/2 cup fresh parsley, chopped

1/3 cup olive oil, lemon-infused if possible

1 pound of pasta

3/4 cup grated Parmesan cheese

salt and pepper to taste

RECIPE:

Put the tomatoes, including skin and seeds, garlic, basil, parsley, olive oil, salt, and pepper in a blender or food processor and blend fully.

Drop pasta in boiling water and cook to the level of softness you like.

Drain and return to the pot. Add the tomato sauce, toss, and serve immediately.

Add grated cheese if you like.

Cals. per serving	Carbs	Fat	Protein
533	73g	20g	17g

DESSERTS

Please bless, O Lord, this chocolate

It's tasty cold, it's tasty hot!

Why, it's even good for you!

(In small amounts—that's also true.)

Mocha, mild and lovely mint,

Chocolate is heaven sent.

So thank You, Blessed, Holy Trinity,

For chocolate made nutt(il)y.

For life, for joys and comforts too—

For all good things that come from you. Amen

Sister of the Society of the Transfiguration

10-Ton Whole Wheat Cake

Serves 10 (Serving size: 1 slice)

Some healthy substitutions were made in this recipe. Stevia, an all-natural, no-calorie sweetener, is derived from a plant source, and replaces the sugar. Other substitutions included canola oil for palm oil, skim milk for whole milk, and non-fat yogurt for regular yogurt. By using these healthier alternatives, you'll save almost 100 calories per serving and cut the carbs in half.

INGREDIENTS:

1½ cup whole wheat flour

1 tablespoon stevia

½ cup applesauce

½ cup wheat germ

3 teaspoons baking powder

½ teaspoon salt

½ cup powdered milk (optional)

½ cup canola oil

2 large eggs

½ cup skim milk

½ cup non-fat yogurt

1 tablespoon vanilla extract or
    ½ tablespoon vanilla extract
    and ½ tablespoon almond extract

RECIPE:

In mixing bowl, combine the flour, stevia, applesauce, wheat germ, baking powder, salt, and powdered milk (if desired).

Stir together to blend, then add oil, eggs, and milk. Mix until dry ingredients are moistened. Beat 1 minute or 100 strokes–just give it a good mix.

Add yogurt and vanilla extract and blend into mixture.

Pour into 2 greased and floured 8-inch cake pans. It tends to be thin. Or, you can pour it all into one and make a single layer. Bake at 350 degrees for 30 to 40 minutes. Test for doneness with a knife. (Let cool and frost with your favorite frosting.)

Cals. per serving	Carbs	Fat	Protein
320	41.5g	14g	7g

Apple and Caramel Crisp

Serves 12 (Serving Size: 1 cup)

The cinnamon in this dish has anti-inflammatory properties, and we added whole wheat flour which has more fiber and nutrients than regular flour.

INGREDIENTS:

Topping

¾ cup old-fashioned oats, uncooked

½ cup butter

½ cup whole wheat flour

1 tablespoon stevia

½ cup Splenda brown sugar

1½ teaspoons cinnamon

¼ teaspoon ground nutmeg

Filling

8 cups (about 3 pounds) tart apples, peeled and sliced thin

½ cup caramel ice cream topping

3 tablespoons flour

2 tablespoons fresh lemon juice

½ cup Splenda brown sugar

¾ teaspoon salt

RECIPE:

Preheat oven to 375 degrees. Grease or butter a glass or ceramic baking dish, about 13 x 9 x 2 inches. Do not use an aluminum baking dish.

In a medium bowl, mix together oats, flour, sugars, cinnamon, nutmeg, and cut in butter until ingredients resemble coarse crumbs. In another bowl, toss apples with caramel topping, flour, lemon juice, brown sugar, and salt. Spread filling evenly into a baking dish. Sprinkle topping over filling.

Bake 45 to 50 minutes. Serve warm with vanilla or cinnamon ice cream.

Cals. per serving	Carbs	Fat	Protein
276	49.5g	8g	1.5g

Banana Carob Chocolate Muffins

Serves 12 (Serving Size: 1 muffin)

Carob tastes similar to chocolate, but has no caffeine and is naturally sweet, low in fat, and high in fiber and calcium. The berry applesauce will add sweetness, as well as nutrition without having to add more sugar. We used whole wheat flour instead of white flour.

INGREDIENTS:

1½ cups whole wheat flour

¼ cup toasted carob powder

1 tablespoon stevia

⅓ cup unsweetened applesauce

1 teaspoon baking soda

½ teaspoon salt

½ teaspoon cinnamon

1 cup mashed overripe banana

4 ounces unsweetened berry applesauce

⅓ cup coconut oil

1 egg

½ cup semi-sweet chocolate chips

½ cup carob chips

RECIPE:

Mix dry ingredients, except for chocolate and carob chips, in a large bowl. Mix wet ingredients in a separate bowl. Make a well in the dry ingredients and add the wet ingredients. Stir until just mixed.

Add chocolate and carob chips and stir until incorporated. Bake in a regular-sized muffin tin at 350 degrees for 20 to 25 minutes or until a toothpick tests clean.

Cals. per serving	Carbs	Fat	Protein
212.5	26.5g	10.5g	3g

Diabetic Strawberry Pie

Serves 8 (Serving Size: 1 slice [1/8 of pie])

We didn't make any changes to the original version of this alternative to high-sugar dessert recipes. You can also just enjoy the fresh strawberries as a dessert by themselves to satisfy your sugar craving. We recommend small portions of sugar-free products, as used is this recipe, because they contain artificial sweeteners whose health consequences are not yet fully understood.

INGREDIENTS:

2 boxes of strawberry flavor sugar-free Jell-O
2 boxes vanilla (cooked) sugar-free pudding
2 quarts fresh strawberries
4 cups water

RECIPE:

Mix pudding with 2 cups of water, stir until thick. Add Jell-O and stir until totally blended, then add the other 2 cups of water. Stir until completely blended.

Slice fresh strawberries and line a pie plate to resemble a pie crust, then pour the strawberry Jell-O mixture over the fresh strawberries.

Cals. per serving	Carbs	Fat	Protein
96.5	20g	0.5g	3g

Healthy Blueberry Banana Muffins

Serves 24 (Serving Size: 1 muffin)

Knowing the average large muffin in a bakery or deli can contain 500 calories or more, we are excited to share this delicious and healthy recipe.

INGREDIENTS:

1½ cups light brown sugar

2 teaspoons baking soda

¾ cup olive oil

2 teaspoons baking powder

2 eggs, well beaten

3 cups whole wheat flour

6 very ripe bananas, mashed

dash of salt

6 tablespoons of 2% milk

2 cups old fashioned oats

2 cups fresh or frozen blueberries

RECIPE:

Combine sugar and oil together, add beaten eggs, mashed bananas, and milk. Mix well.

Sift flour with baking soda, baking powder, and salt. Add to the wet ingredients.

Mix in the oats, then stir in the blueberries.

Fill muffin tins ¾ full using non-stick pans or line with parchment paper. Bake at 350 degrees for 20 minutes. They should be golden brown.

Cals. per serving	Carbs	Fat	Protein
200	28g	8g	4g

Native American Pumpkin Bread

Serves 8 (Serving Size: 7 ounces)

INGREDIENTS:

1½ cups Splenda*

¾ cup whole wheat flour

½ cup vegetable oil

1 teaspoon salt

2 eggs

1 teaspoon baking powder

½ teaspoon baking soda

1 cup canned pumpkin puree

½ cup raisins

⅓ cup water

½ cup chopped walnuts

1¼ cup all-purpose flour

½ teaspoon each of allspice, cinnamon, ground cloves, and nutmeg

*For a natural alternative, replace with 3 tablespoons of stevia (powder or liquid). For every one cup of sugar that is replaced by stevia, there should be ⅓ cup of a liquid or other "bulk" added to the recipe, i.e. applesauce.

RECIPE:

Preheat oven to 350 degrees. Grease a 9 x 5 inch loaf pan.

Combine the Splenda (or stevia), oil, eggs, pumpkin, and water. Mix to incorporate.

In a separate bowl, combine flours, salt, baking soda, baking powder, and spices.

Add to liquid ingredients and stir until moistened. Fold in raisins and walnuts.

Pour into pan and bake for 1 hour. Use toothpick to test for doneness. Remove from pan and cool completely.

Cals. per serving	Carbs	Fat	Protein
239.5	25g	13.5g	4.5g

Great Spirit, we ask you to

Come and bless this meal we

Are about to eat, and bless all

Of us gathered together in your name.

Amen.

Peaches with Blackberry Sauce

Serves 4 (Serving Size: 1 cup)

Blackberries contain antioxidants called antho-cyanins which are believed to protect against cancer and offer heart health benefits. Raw cane sugar is used because it is not bleached.

INGREDIENTS:

1 cup blackberries

2 tablespoons raw cane sugar

3 teaspoons fresh lemon juice

4 large ripe peaches, peeled and sliced

4 small mint leaves for garnish

RECIPE:

Combine the blackberries, sugar, and 1 teaspoon of the lemon juice in a food processor. Puree until smooth. To remove seeds, pass the puree through a fine sieve into a bowl. Cover and refrigerate the blackberry sauce for at least 2 hours.

To serve, spoon about 1½ tablespoons of the sauce over the bottom of 4 dessert dishes. Toss the peach slices with the remaining lemon juice and arrange attractively on top. Garnish with mint.

Cals. per serving	Carbs	Fat	Protein
117	25g	1g	2g

Ali's Oatmeal Chocolate Chip Peanut Butter Whole Wheat Cookies

Serves: 50 (Serving Size: 1 cookie)

INGREDIENTS:

1½ cups quick cooking oats

1½ cups whole wheat flour

1 teaspoon baking soda

1 teaspoon cinnamon

1 cup unsalted butter

¾ cup granulated sugar

¾ cup packed brown sugar

2 teaspoons vanilla extract

½ cup natural peanut butter

2 eggs

1 (10-ounce) package chocolate chips

RECIPE:

Preheat oven to 375 degrees.

In a large bowl, combine oats, whole wheat flour, baking soda, and cinnamon. Set aside.

Melt the butter and then combine with sugar, brown sugar, vanilla extract, peanut butter, and eggs.

Add the dry ingredients to the wet ingredients; when well mixed, stir in the chocolate chips.

Drop rounded teaspoons onto greased cookie sheets, about 1 inch apart from each other.

Bake at 375 degrees for 10 minutes. Cookies will be golden brown when done.

When cookies are done, let them cool on the baking pan for one minute. Then move cookies to wire rack to cool completely.

Cals. per serving	Carbs	Fat	Protein
131	14.2g	8g	2.4g

COFFEE HOUR

Bread Ministry

For loaves of bread, of corn and wheat
Of rye and millet, pastries sweet,
Of every sort of bread we eat
We give you thanks, Oh Lord.

For with great bounty you sustain
Our mortal bodies with this grain
That grows in sunshine, soil, and rain
We give you thanks, Oh Lord.

Our spirits feed on wine and bread,
The Mysteries of the life you led.
Eternally our souls are fed.
We give you thanks, Oh Lord.

And with the breads we gladly share
May You be present with your care
And touch those lives with comfort fair.
We give you thanks, Oh Lord.

Sandy Davis

Walnut and Cocoa Muffins

Serves 12 (Serving Size: 1 muffin)

INGREDIENTS:

2 whole eggs

1½ cups whole wheat flour

1 egg white

⅓ teaspoon baking soda

½ cup Splenda brown sugar*

½ cup cocoa powder (unsweetened)

⅓ cup vegetable oil

⅓ cup low-fat buttermilk

½ cup unsweetened applesauce

½ cup chopped walnuts

*For a natural alternative, replace with 3 tablespoons of stevia (powder or liquid). For every one cup of sugar that is replaced by stevia, there should be ⅓ cup of a liquid or other "bulk" added to the recipe, i.e. applesauce.

RECIPE:

Preheat oven to 350 degrees. Lightly oil or spray muffin tin.

Beat eggs and sugar until thick and creamy. Gradually add oil and then applesauce.

Sift together flour, baking soda, and cocoa powder.

Fold half of the flour mixture into the eggs. Stir in buttermilk and then fold in remaining flour mixture. Add walnuts and blend into batter.

Spoon into prepared muffin pan and bake 15 to 20 minutes or until a toothpick comes out clean.

Cals. per serving	Carbs	Fat	Protein
177	15g	11g	4.5g

Bran Muffins

Serves 12 (Serving Size: 1 muffin)

INGREDIENTS:

1 cup unprocessed wheat bran

1 cup low-fat buttermilk

2 large eggs

¼ cup unsweetened applesauce

2 tablespoons molasses

2 tablespoons honey

1 cup white flour

½ cup whole wheat flower

2 teaspoons baking powder

1 teaspoon baking soda

½ teaspoon salt

½ teaspoon cinnamon

2 tablespoons Splenda*

1 cup blueberries

*For a natural alternative, replace with 1½ teaspoons stevia (powder or liquid).

RECIPE:

Place bran in a large bowl with buttermilk and stir. Leave for 30 minutes to soften. Beat eggs with whisk and add to bran. Add applesauce, molasses, and honey and stir to combine. Gently fold in blueberries.

In a small bowl combine flours, baking powder, soda, salt, cinnamon, and sweetener. Add to wet mixture and combine just until mixed. Don't overbeat.

Spray muffin tin with non-stick spray and divide batter evenly into muffin cups.

Bake at 375 degrees for 12 minutes or until toothpick inserted into center of one muffin comes out clean. Remove from tins to cool.

Note: for the molasses and honey, spray a ¼ cup measure with non-stick spray. Fill it halfway with honey and top off with molasses. Then use the same measure for the applesauce.

A small jar of baby applesauce or even prunes is the right amount for this recipe.

Use whatever fruit you have around: chopped apples, chunks of firm peaches, even sliced grapes. A favorite combination is cranberries and blueberries. Cut the cranberries in half if they're large. Or add dried cranberries or raisins to any of the above.

Cals. per serving	Carbs	Fat	Protein
186.5	35g	2.5g	6g

Energy Boost Bars

Serves 10 (makes ten 1½-ounce bars)

INGREDIENTS:

8-ounce bag whole almonds

1½ cup quick oats

1 cup dried blueberries

1 teaspoon cinnamon

¼ cup sesame seeds

½ cup dried cranberries

⅔ cup sugar-free maple syrup

cooking spray

Cals per serving	Carbs	Fat	Protein
263	29g	13g	7.5g

RECIPE

Preheat oven to 275 degrees. Lightly grease a 9-inch baking pan with cooking spray. In a food processor, grind almonds until they resemble coarse meal. Combine the ground almonds and the remaining ingredients in a large bowl. Stir until well blended. Using wet fingers, press mixture into the prepared pan. Bake for 1 hour. Cool in pan on a wire rack.

Slice into bars, and store in airtight container.

Saint Raphael's Oakhurst Sunday Quiche

Serves 20 (makes two 9-inch quiches) (Serving Size: 1/10 of quiche)

This revised and healthier version of the original recipe decreases the total calories by 204 and cuts the fat in half by substituting ham for sausage and light sour cream for whipped cream. We also decreased the saturated fat by substituting olive oil for butter and used low-fat cheese, which makes the dish more heart healthy. You can also use egg replacers for the whole eggs to save on more calories and fat.

Cals. per serving	Carbs	Fat	Protein
452	18g	26g	36.5g

INGREDIENTS:

2 (7-ounce) packages sliced ham

1 chopped onion

1 red bell pepper red

1 pound mushrooms, sliced

2 pounds fresh asparagus

3 tablespoons olive oil

1½ pounds of 2%-fat shredded cheese of your choice

1 package pie crust (2 [9-inch] crusts per package)

1 teaspoon salt

1 teaspoon pepper

1 teaspoon nutmeg

20 eggs

2 cups light sour cream

RECIPE:

Steam the asparagus or broccoli until tender and set aside.

Sauté the onion and bell pepper in olive oil until limp and then add the mushrooms until they change color.

Cut the ham into bite-sized pieces. The ham does not have to be cooked.

Mix the sautéed vegetables, the steamed vegetables, and the meat.

Mix (slightly whipping) the eggs, pepper, salt, nutmeg, and sour cream. Add a handful of the shredded cheese and mix.

Put the pie shells in the bottom of two 9 x 12-inch glass pans and add the mixed vegetables and meat in the pans with the remaining cheese on top.

Pour the egg mixture over the other ingredients and put in the refrigerator, covered. Bake at 350 degrees for 1 hour.

Grace before Meals

For food in a world where many walk in hunger,
For faith in a world where many walk in fear,
For friends in a world where many walk alone,
We offer you our grateful thanks, O Lord.

The Rev. Jane F. Flaherty

St. Timothy's Coffee Cake

Serves 12 (Serving Size: 1 slice)

This dessert is well received with either raisins or dried cranberries in the batter. This is a healthier cake than some because it uses a sugar substitute and fat-free sour cream. We thought we could make it even better by replacing the artificial sweetener and margarine with healthier alternatives.

We replaced the Splenda, an artificial sweetener, with stevia, a no-calorie natural sweetener made from a plant extract.

We also substituted canola oil for margarine, which contains trans fats to keep them solid and increase cholesterol and the risk of heart disease. The substitution didn't change the calories much, but it made this a healthier cake.

INGREDIENTS:

½ cup canola oil

¼ teaspoon salt

2 cups Splenda*

1 teaspoon cinnamon

½ teaspoon vanilla extract

1 cup chopped walnuts

2 eggs

½ cup golden raisins

2 cups unsifted all-purpose flour

1 cup fat-free sour cream

1 teaspoon baking powder

4 teaspoons cinnamon sugar

* For a natural alternative, use 2 tablespoons stevia (powder or liquid). For every one cup of sugar that is replaced by stevia, there should be ⅓ cup of a liquid or other "bulk" added to the recipe, i.e. applesauce.

RECIPE:

Combine Splenda (or stevia), oil, and vanilla, and blend. Add eggs, one at a time, beating well after each.

Sift together flour, baking powder, salt, and cinnamon. Add nuts and raisins; coat well. Add dry ingredients to the wet mixture, alternating with sour cream. Blend well.

Pour into a greased and floured Bundt pan. Sprinkle with cinnamon sugar.

Bake in a 350-degree oven—60 minutes for a small Bundt pan and 1½ hours for a large Bundt pan, or until the cake tests done. Leave in pan for at least 1 hour before turning out.

Turn out and sprinkle with more cinnamon sugar.

Cals. per serving	Carbs	Fat	Protein
324	30g	20g	6g

"And having food and raiment let us be therewith content."

I Timothy 6:8

Scrambled Egg Muffins

Serves 12 (Serving Size: 1 muffin)

Only use the egg whites from 6 of the eggs rather than 12 whole eggs, ham rather than a fattier meat like sausage, and reduced-fat cheese to make a healthier dish.

INGREDIENTS:

½ pound cooked ham

6 whole eggs

6 egg whites

½ cup onion, chopped

½ cup green pepper, chopped

½ teaspoon salt

¼ teaspoon pepper

¼ teaspoon garlic powder

½ cup fat-free shredded cheddar cheese

RECIPE:

Chop the ham, onions, and green pepper and set aside. If using sausage, brown the sausage in a skillet and drain. Skip this step if using ham.

In a bowl, beat the eggs (and whites), add onions, green pepper, salt, pepper, and garlic powder. Stir in browned sausage (or ham) and cheese. Fill greased muffin cups ⅓ full.

Bake at 350 degrees for 20 to 25 minutes or until a knife inserted near the center comes out clean.

Cals. per serving	Carbs	Fat	Protein
99	2.5g	5g	11g

POTLUCK

Prayer for all who make our meals possible

Pour Your richest blessing, O Lord, we pray

On those whose hard work allow us to eat.

For those who plant and care for the land

We ask your blessing

For those whose sweat and aching backs harvest the crops,

We ask your blessing

For those who package and transport the food,

We ask your blessing

For those stockers and checkers and all in the stores,

We ask your blessing

For thousand not named, whom only you know,

We ask your blessing

For this food, for all who made it possible and for us as we gather together,

We ask your blessing and offer heartfelt thanksgiving.

Sr. Diana

Marinated Corn and Zucchini Salad

Serves 10 (Serving Size: ²/₃ cup)

Want to save more calories and make this salad even healthier? Eliminate the sugar. You'll get enough sweetness from the corn, onion, and peppers. You can also substitute the sugar with calorie-free stevia, an all-natural sweetener from a plant extract. You can find it in powder or liquid form online or in many stores. Caution: it's very sweet, so use only 4 teaspoons of powder or several drops of the liquid form to replace the sugar.

INGREDIENTS:

2 cups frozen sweet corn kernels

1 small sweet onion (such as Vidalia)

2 medium zucchini

1 medium red bell pepper

½ cup chopped parsley, loosely packed

⅓ cup water

⅓ cup sugar

⅓ cup vinegar (fruit, red wine, or apple cider)

2 tablespoons olive oil

½ teaspoon coarse ground black pepper

½ teaspoon salt

RECIPE:

Pour corn into a colander and rinse thoroughly with cool water to begin defrosting. Drain well and place in a large bowl. Peel and finely chop the onion and add it to the bowl.

Cut the zucchini into bite-size pieces and add it to the bowl. Rinse and seed the bell pepper. Cut it into bite-size pieces and add it and the chopped parsley to the bowl.

In a 2 cup measuring glass, microwave the water and sugar, uncovered, on high for 45 seconds. Whisk the mixture until the sugar dissolves. Whisk in the vinegar, oil, pepper, and salt. Pour the dressing over the vegetables and stir to coat well.

Refrigerate, covered, for at least an hour or up to 2 days.

Cals. per serving	Carbs	Fat	Protein
88.5	19g	0.5g	2g

Baked Spaghetti

Serves 10 (Serving Size: 1½ cup)

In this recipe we made a few revisions to the original submission. We replaced the butter and saturated fat with heart-healthy, mono-unsaturated fat from extra virgin olive oil, even leaner ground beef that's grass-fed, 98% fat-free condensed mushroom soup, fat-free cheddar cheese, and whole wheat pasta. These changes decreased the saturated fat which is linked to heart disease; lowered the calories that can help reduce weight; increased fiber that can fight cancer; and used products that are environmentally friendly. To make this dish meat free, omit the ground beef.

INGREDIENTS:

olive oil cooking spray

1 cup onion, chopped

1 cup green pepper, chopped

2¼ teaspoons extra virgin olive oil

1 (28-ounce) can tomatoes with liquid

1 (4-ounce) can mushrooms stems and pieces, drained

2 teaspoons dried oregano

1 teaspoon dried basil

1 teaspoon garlic powder

1 cup dry white wine

1 pound 95% lean ground beef, browned and drained

12 ounces whole wheat angel hair spaghetti, cooked and drained

2 cups shredded fat-free sharp cheddar cheese, divided

1 can condensed 98% fat-free cream of mushroom soup

¼ cup water

½ cup grated Parmesan cheese, divided

RECIPE:

In a medium skillet lightly coated with cooking spray, brown the beef, drain off liquid, and set aside.

Follow directions on the box for cooking the angel hair spaghetti. When finished, drain and set aside. In a large skillet or Dutch Oven, over medium heat, sauté onions and green pepper in olive oil until tender. Add tomatoes, mushrooms, oregano, basil, garlic powder, and white wine. Add ground beef. Simmer uncovered for 20 minutes.

Place half of the cooked spaghetti in a 13 x 9 x 2–inch baking dish, lightly coated with cooking spray. Top with half of the vegetable mixture. Sprinkle with 1 cup cheddar cheese and ¼ cup Parmesan cheese. Repeat layers.

Mix the soup and water until smooth, pour and spread over casserole. Sprinkle with remaining Parmesan cheese.

Bake uncovered at 350 degrees for 35 to 45 minutes or until heated through.

Freezes well. Reheat in microwave or oven.

Cals. per serving	Carbs	Fat	Protein
306.5	39g	6.5g	23g

Mayo-less Coleslaw

Serves 10 (Serving Size: ¾ cup)

This is a healthy alternative to coleslaw that is typically swimming in mayonnaise. Packed with cabbage, which is believed to have cancer-fighting agents, this dish only contains 9 calories of fat per serving compared to the 150 to 200 calories of traditional mayonnaise-based coleslaw.

INGREDIENTS:

½ pound green cabbage, shredded to make about 2 cups

½ pound red cabbage, shredded to make about 2 cups

½ pound napa cabbage or spinach, about 2 cups

1 cup red onions, thinly sliced

½ cup green onions, chopped

½ cup cilantro, chopped

¾ cup olive oil

¼ cup cider vinegar

2 teaspoons honey

½ cup whole grain mustard

1 tablespoon garlic, minced

1 tablespoon salt

1 tablespoon freshly ground black pepper

1 teaspoon cayenne pepper

RECIPE:

Place the green cabbage, red cabbage, napa cabbage or spinach, red onions, green onions, and cilantro in a large salad bowl.

In a small bowl, whisk the olive oil, vinegar, honey, mustard, garlic, salt, black pepper, and cayenne pepper. Mix well. Add the mixture to the greens and toss to mix thoroughly.

Cover and refrigerate for at least one hour. Serve chilled.

Cals. per serving	Carbs	Fat	Protein
198	8g	18g	1g

Meringue Cookies

Serves 65 (Serving size: 1 cookie)

This recipe uses dark chocolate instead of milk chocolate, which can help lower blood pressure. Splenda is used to save calories, and there is an even healthier alternative below. Pecans, in moderation, are a good source of vitamin E.

INGREDIENTS:

2 egg whites

¾ cup Splenda*

½ teaspoon vanilla extract

¾ cup chopped pecans

1 cup dark chocolate chips

*For a natural alternative, replace with 1½ tablespoons stevia (powder or liquid).

RECIPE:

Beat together egg whites, Splenda, and vanilla until stiff and then fold in the chopped pecans and dark chocolate chips.

Drop by spoonfuls on a foil-covered cookie sheet. Place in oven at 450 degrees and then turn oven off immediately. Leave in oven overnight (no less than 4 hours).

Cals. per serving	Carbs	Fat	Protein
27	2.5g	2g	0.5g

Fresh Peach and Blueberry Cobbler

Serves 10 (Serving Size: ¾ cup)

Peaches are high in potassium which can help lower blood pressure, and blueberries contain anthocyanin antioxidants that reduce inflammation and can fight disease. We are using Smart Balance Buttery Spread as an alternative to margarine. This spread has no added trans or hyrogenated fats and lots of omega-3s, which are healthy and fight disease. The walnuts also contain omega-3s and are one of the healthiest nuts. Cinnamon fights inflammation, and oatmeal is a great source of carbohydrate with no sugar added.

INGREDIENTS:

Filling

4 cups fresh peeled, sliced peaches
2 cups fresh blueberries
⅓ cup Splenda brown sugar*
1 tablespoon cornstarch
1 tablespoon lemon juice
1 tablespoon cinnamon
1 tablespoon almond or vanilla extract

Topping

1¼ cup quick-cooking oatmeal
½ cup flour
¼ cup Splenda brown sugar*
¾ cup chopped walnuts
¼ cup Smart Balance Buttery Spread Original

*For a natural alternative, replace with 1 tablespoon stevia (powder or liquid). For every 1 cup of sugar that is replaced by stevia there should be a ⅓ cup of a liquid or other "bulk" added to the recipe, ie. applesauce.

RECIPE:

Combine peaches, blueberries, brown sugar, vanilla extract, and cinnamon in a saucepan over medium heat. Bring to a boil, stirring occasionally.

Combine cornstarch and lemon juice and add to peach mixture, stirring well.

Bring to a boil again and remove from heat. Pour into a greased casserole dish or pie plate. Combine all topping ingredients and sprinkle over fruit mixture.

Bake at 350 degrees for 30 to 45 minutes or until bubbly and topping is slightly browned.

Cals. per serving	Carbs	Fat	Protein
267	42.5g	9g	4g

NetWork's Bar-B-Que Beef for Sandwiches

Serves 11 (Serving Size: 1 cup)

For this recipe, we suggest using a very lean and trimmed chuck roast. We were also able to cut back on the sugar by reducing the amount of ketchup.

INGREDIENTS:

1 (4-pound) lean chuck roast, trimmed
    of all visible fat
1 medium onion, chopped
1 teaspoon celery salt
1 teaspoon Worcestershire sauce
½ teaspoon Tabasco sauce
¼ teaspoon garlic powder
1 tablespoon chili powder
1 cup water
6 ounces ketchup
⅓ cup light brown sugar

RECIPE:

Place meat in roasting pan. Combine the other ingredients and pour over the meat. Bake, covered, for 6 hours at 250 degrees. This can also be done in a large crock pot. Shred the meat with forks and remove any bones or fat. Stir and serve on buns. Freezes well.

Cals. per serving	Carbs	Fat	Protein
323	17.1g	10.2g	41g

Lord God, this is the first time I have prepared a Meal for so many people, please guide me along The way and may Your will be done. If the meal is Delicious, may I grow in gratitude; and if it is a Disaster, please help me grow in humility. For Your Grace, I pray. Amen

The Sisters of the Society of the Transfiguration

99

Roast Turkey

Serves 8 (Serving Size: 6 ounces)

INGREDIENTS:

1 turkey, 14 to 20 pounds

4 carrots

4 celery stalks

2 onions

1¼ sticks of butter at room temperature

2 tablespoons parsley (preferably fresh)

2 tablespoons sage (preferably fresh)

2 tablespoons rosemary (preferably fresh)

2 tablespoons thyme (preferably fresh)

4–8 cups chicken stock

Cals. per serving	Carbs	Fat	Protein
476	7g	30g	40g

RECIPE:

Put half of veggies under turkey in roaster and the other half inside the turkey. Put butter and herbs in a food processor and mix till blended. Rub butter mixture on all exposed areas of the turkey.

Place in 450-degree oven for 45 minutes. Reduce heat to 350 degrees and cook for 1¼ hours basting turkey every 15 minutes with warm chicken stock. The turkey is done when the meat thermometer reaches 185 degrees Fahrenheit.

Remove turkey to serving platter, tent with foil and let it rest—20 minutes for a bird up to 20 pounds and 40 minutes for a bird over that.